"Blair Imani enlivens African American history for a new generation with her dynamic and thoughtful account of African American migration and resilience."

—JAMIA WILSON, EXECUTIVE DIRECTOR AND PUBLISHER OF FEMINIST PRESS

"In this painstakingly crafted and researched tome, the beauty and purpose of the Great Migration comes alive in ways that reawaken our connection to our community. This is definitely one to add to your library of thoughtful, thought-provoking history books."

—VANESSA DE LUCA, EDITOR-IN-CHIEF AT *ZORA* MAGAZINE BY MEDIUM

"*Making Our Way Home* takes you on a riveting journey through the history of African American migration. Blair Imani crafts a poignant narrative that is an accessible, enjoyable, and valuable contribution to our people's history. The colorful imagery, lesser-known moments, and powerful statements on our tenacity and fortitude come together in a beautiful work of art."

—FEMINISTA JONES, ACTIVIST AND AUTHOR OF *RECLAIMING OUR SPACE*

"Lively, highly readable, and beautifully illustrated, *Making Our Way Home* is a wonderful primer on the Great Migration and African American life between 1910 and 1979."

—DR. STEPHEN FINLEY, DIRECTOR OF AFRICAN AND AFRICAN AMERICAN STUDIES AT LOUISIANA STATE UNIVERSITY

"There's something revolutionary about recounting our history, especially since traditional narratives often reflect only a sliver of the full Black American experience. But in the tradition of African griots, *Making Our Way Home* carries on the legacy of our fore-parents, informing new generations about how we got to where we are, and how America—and the world—was transformed in the process."

—TRE'VELL ANDERSON, DIRECTOR OF CULTURE AND ENTERTAINMENT AT *OUT* MAGAZINE

MAKING OUR WAY HOME

MAKING OUR WAY HOME

The Great Migration and the Black American Dream

Blair Imani

Foreword by Patrisse Cullors

Illustrations by Rachelle Baker

TEN SPEED PRESS

California | New York

CONTENTS

FOREWORD

Forty-nine years after the Emancipation Proclamation, Jennie Endsley was born in Texarkana, Arkansas. She was the daughter of a Black and Chickasaw medicine man, and would eventually become a math teacher. She grew up during the terror of the Ku Klux Klan, and remembered her father firing warning shots when the Klan would come to their home and threaten to burn it down. We now know that the Klan created an environment of terror for Black communities, which contributed to a mass migration out of the South. Jennie's time in Arkansas came to an end when her brothers made a plan to send her west to Los Angeles, California, for her own safety. Jennie Endsley was my grandmother.

Jennie and her only son spent their first decade in California in Ramona Gardens, a housing project in East Los Angeles. Her first husband was murdered in an incident about which I know very little. Louise "Fox" Endsley, my grandmother's second husband, was a World War II veteran and one of the few Black men who benefited from the G.I. Bill. Because of this, the family was able to move from South Central Los Angeles to Pacoima, a neighborhood in the San Fernando Valley that was one of the only areas open to Black homeowners. While Jim Crow laws were pervasive in the Southern states, there was more subtle segregation, in the form of redlining, occurring in places such as Los Angeles. Even though it was highly segregated in terms of housing, the San Fernando Valley was still a melting pot of cultures as a home to survivors of Japanese internment, Black folks fleeing the terror of the South, a rising Mexican immigrant population, and affluent white communities.

Making Our Way Home offers a clear and concise look at why so many of our ancestors made the move to the North and West. The Great Migration is a story of triumph and despair, and offers an opportunity to examine the most important time in American history: Post-Reconstruction to the Civil Rights movement. Black Americans have spent a significant amount of time and energy attempting to repair the harm caused to us by a multilayered system that branded us as three-fifths human. To this day, we see the repercussions of that compromise.

With the help of her family, my grandmother fled a violent and bloody South and made her way in a liberal Los Angeles. She created a new space for herself, believing that the West held a promise that was never afforded to her father. She was mostly right. She made a way from no way, and my entire family benefited from it.

I am grateful to Blair Imani for reminding us that history gives us the true calling toward our freedom. We can't change what we don't understand, but we *can* change what we acknowledge. May this book be a reminder of the sacrifices made by the generations before us that were forced to flee their homes and make new lives in new places. I love you, grandmother. I love you, Jennie Endsley.

—Patrisse Cullors

INTRODUCTION

Growing up, I often wondered what had happened during the years between the end of chattel slavery and the start of the Civil Rights movement. I often joked that Black people disappeared from the face of the earth during World War I and World War II only to return with music, afros, and righteous indignation in the late 1950s. In reality, Black Americans have been present throughout every chapter of American history, having served in every war in which America was involved and contributing to the culture, economy, and very identity of the United States. To put it plainly, the story of America is incomplete if it is told absent the story of Black America. That truth may feel very obvious to us, but the creators and curators of many American history courses, textbooks, museums, and works of media frequently ignore this vast community and its myriad contributions. When history reflects only white men and their victories, it becomes difficult for everyone else to feel as if they, too, can be victorious. Very few Americans are even aware that over six million Black people moved across the United States from 1910 to 1979 in a period known as the Great Migration. Perhaps you learned about the Great Migration from family accounts, history class, or Isabel Wilkerson's foundational text *The Warmth of Other Suns*. Perhaps you are just now learning about it.

During the Great Migration, Black Americans surfed the cresting waves of a cultural crescendo. Not only did we move—in 1910, Detroit had a population of 5,700 Black people, which boomed to 120,000 less than thirty years later—we told our stories and rallied against the notion of shame in our Blackness. White society changed our names from slurs to Coloreds to Negros to Afro-Americans to Blacks. We wrote books. We made art. We made music. We fought. We lost. We won. We survived. We made history.

Some historians separate the Great Migration into two waves: the first Great Migration, which lasted from 1910 to 1930 and ended with the Great Depression, and the second Great Migration, which started during the industrialization of World War II and ended in the late 1970s. For the purposes of this book, I will be discussing these two periods as one Great Migration.

Seeking a better future, millions of Black families uprooted themselves from the rich soil of the American South and relocated to the hardened asphalt and cobblestone streets of the North, Midwest, and West. Our families did this in a time before cell phones, the Internet, and global positioning systems. They did it as the racist specter of Jim Crow made it uncertain if they could even fill their trucks with the much-needed gasoline and food to fuel their journeys. But not all of them moved away. Many families stayed in cities like Houston, New Orleans, Jacksonville, and Atlanta, deciding, "Better the devil you know than the devil you don't"—or, in other words, preferring to endure familiar racism and discrimination than find themselves uprooted and still at war with the devil of racism in another city.

For the six million individuals who did move, such a decision was not made on a whim. Extensive research and interviews reveal that there were two primary reasons families migrated during this time period: to pursue jobs and to seek refuge from domestic terrorism. Economic hardship down South and the promise of jobs up North drew Black people to new cities like Detroit, New York, and Chicago. Pillars of American capitalism relied on Black newcomers from the South to maintain the output of automobiles and building materials that were fueling America's rapid industrial growth. Unfortunately, these families that moved north and left the sharecropping fields for the assembly lines encountered horrific working conditions and endured long working hours.

My own family moved from Little Rock, Arkansas, to Los Angeles, California, following the lynching of Willie Kees in 1936. Lynchings had become an extremely common form of mass intimidation, and following this particular lynching, the Ku Klux Klan threatened any Black person who dared to resume their daily routine. My great-grandfather, Vernon Dunlap, whom I knew as Big Daddy, defiantly went to work the day following the lynching despite the threat of violence from white supremacists. He was spotted on his way to work and, faced with the threat of being lynched himself, he was forced to leave his young family behind and headed west in the dead of night. About a month later, Big Daddy was able to settle in California.

Shortly thereafter, he returned to Little Rock on a mission to evacuate his whole community and bring them as refugees to the promised land.

Many accounts of Black American history characterize our past as being shaped by hardship and suffering alone. While these are valid and sacred parts of our story, the historical record reveals that our legacies have been shaped by far more than pain and suffering. *Making Our Way Home* is a primer on the Great Migration for people of all ages and cultural heritages. Chapter one covers the post–Civil War period known as Reconstruction to 1919, and subsequent chapters each cover a decade of the Great Migration, providing an overview of the cultural changes that were occurring in America.

Black history is so much more than the snapshots that white institutions allow us to hold on to. It is time we pull away the cover obscuring the rich history of Black America during what has come to be known as the Great Migration. From the time of Reconstruction to the birth of hip-hop, millions of Black Americans moved across—and fundamentally changed—the United States to forge a better future.

SEPARATE BUT EQUAL
RECONSTRUCTION—1919

BY THE TURN OF THE TWENTIETH CENTURY, THE UNITED STATES had proved that it was essentially opposed to properly protecting and supporting Black Americans. This opposition became evident through a series of events that took place after the Civil War. By the war's end, the Emancipation Proclamation, which was issued by President Abraham Lincoln on January 1, 1863, marked the beginning of the end for chattel slavery in the United States. The proclamation was not all-encompassing, however; it only applied to the Confederate States, which had seceded from the Union, meaning that those states that had participated in slavery but did not leave the Union were not obligated to free enslaved people. Texas, where the proclamation should have applied, did not even recognize this liberatory order until more than two years later, on June 19, 1865, a day that is still celebrated by many Black Americans as an independence day called Juneteenth. The ratification of the Thirteenth Amendment to the U.S. Constitution in December 1865 freed the remaining enslaved people (except those enslaved as a punishment for crime). But the legacy of chattel slavery, combined with the anti-Blackness that has come to define American racism, meant that even free Black people were viewed as subhuman objects to be controlled. And with no reparations to account for a dearth of financial resources, formal education programs, or job opportunities to facilitate growth and progress, conditions for Black Americans were slow to improve. But as is often said of the Black community, we made a way out of no way and created our own infrastructure of support.

RECONSTRUCTION

In the years that immediately followed the Civil War, known collectively as Reconstruction, a steady rhythm of progress echoed throughout the United States. It was an ambitious undertaking to retrofit the institutions that had allowed slavery to prosper with new features that could provide for the protection of America's marginalized. The Freedmen's Bureau, which was first established by President Lincoln in 1865, worked alongside Black people across the South to build schools and replace the system of enforced illiteracy with literacy programs. Starting in 1867, the Reconstruction acts laid out terms of reentry into the Union for the states that had seceded during the Civil War.

Until new state constitutions could be drafted and approved by the U.S. Congress, the former confederacy was divided into five districts, each governed by military leaders. Laws were also established to allow men of all races, with the exception of former Confederate leaders, to participate in the creation of those new constitutions. Further protections were enacted in the form of the Fourteenth and Fifteenth Amendments. The Fourteenth Amendment defined an American citizen as any person born in or "naturalized" in the United States. This amendment also overturned the U.S. Supreme Court's decision in the *Dred Scott* case (1857), which had ruled that Black people were not eligible for citizenship. The Fifteenth Amendment prohibited state, local, and federal governments from denying U.S. citizens the right to vote based on race, color, or past servitude, thus extending

Pierre Caliste Landry

Hiram Rhodes Revels

voting rights to Black men. (It's notable that these new protections did not extend to Native Americans, who were not granted citizenship until 1924 with the passage of the Snyder Act.) The Reconstruction acts and the new amendments slowly provided a path forward for Black people to participate in the country's governance.

From 1863 to 1877, approximately 1,500 Black men, many of whom were born enslaved, became the first Black Americans elected or appointed to positions on the federal, state, and local level. Pierre Caliste Landry, born enslaved in 1841, was sold away from his family at the age of thirteen for under $2,000, or just over $60,000 in today's dollars. Likely due to his privilege as a light-skinned, mixed-race Black person, Landry had been able to pursue an education during his adolescence and into adulthood despite being enslaved. When the Thirteenth Amendment freed enslaved people, Landry opened schools for Black children, who were now free to attain literacy as well as a general education. He became a prominent member of the community in Donaldsonville, Louisiana, where he was elected mayor in 1868, making him the first Black mayor of a U.S. city. Landry went on to found a Historically Black College or University (HBCU) in Louisiana, which was renamed Dillard University, in 1935. There were other prominent civic leaders during this time who were the descendants of freed Black people. Hiram Rhodes Revels, who had never been enslaved, served as a Mississippi senator and became the first Black member to serve in the U.S. Congress in 1870. P. B. S. Pinchback, also a free man, served as governor of Louisiana after the former governor

P. B. S. Pinchback

was suspended from office in 1872. Although Pinchback served for only four weeks, he was the only African American governor of a U.S. state for 118 years until 1990, when Douglas Wilder was elected governor of Virginia and became the second.

Under President Ulysses S. Grant, the U.S. military was charged with enforcing the laws that allowed Black people to establish themselves after centuries of enslavement. Another protection was established by the Civil Rights Act of 1875, which prohibited discrimination in public accommodations and in jury selection. Progress appeared to be on the horizon, but America's nineteenth president, Rutherford B. Hayes, ensured that any glimmer of hope was just a mirage. In 1877, following his inauguration, President Hayes's first major act was to bring the Reconstruction era to a close by reducing the presence of the federal government and reinvigorating states' rights. Under the Reconstruction acts, states had been forced to include Black men in the affairs of the state. But under President Hayes, the protections outlined in the Reconstruction and Enforcement acts were effectively moot, leaving Black people without recourse against hate groups and discrimination. Although Hayes was a Republican (the more liberal party at the time), he happily accommodated the wishes of conservative white Southern Democrats, who sought to maintain the system of white supremacy that excluded Black people from public life. As a result, the South was free to resurrect the pre–Civil War way of life, where rather than Black people being enslaved, they became second-class citizens.

Lynching was one of the most horrific products of the period after Reconstruction. The majority of lynchings in America took place between 1890 and the 1920s and happened in the South, where most Black people lived. Historians have diligently worked to catalog these atrocities, but it is likely that not all of the lynching victims were recorded. Estimates from the Tuskegee Institute place the number of people lynched between 1882 and 1968 at 4,743 people, 72 percent of whom were African Americans. According to extensive historical research from the Equal Justice Initiative, 4,084 African Americans were lynched between 1877 and 1950 in the South. In 1892, at the peak of the lynching epidemic, Black journalist Ida B. Wells launched a campaign to expose the brutalities of lynching. Wells gained national recognition with her publication of a bold exposé on the

Ida B. Wells

lynching of three Black men named Will Stewart, Tommie Moss, and Calvin McDowell in Memphis, Tennessee. While the men had been accused of sexually harassing a white woman, Wells revealed that a more credible impetus for their murders was their economic competition with local white grocery store owners. Her work culminated in her book *The Red Record*, which was published in 1895 and became the foundation for much of the research into lynching and prompted the recording of the names of lynching victims. In a time well before social media, Ida B. Wells chronicled and exposed the indignities suffered by the Black community in print. Before his death, Frederick Douglass praised Wells's journalism as "a revelation of existing conditions." Her work informed countless emerging leaders, and her contributions continue to shape Black feminist theory more than a century later.

Jim Crow laws proliferated across the former Confederacy with the aim of keeping white people separate from people of color and ensuring that people of color lived as second-class citizens. This segregation extended to education, transportation, health care, commerce, marriage, adoption, voting, and more. The laws also used slavery-era language to classify Black people by their connections to whiteness. People with mixed heritage that included white ancestry were called mulatto or, based on the fraction of their Black and white heritage, as quadroon or octoroon. Under Jim Crow, these designations afforded privileges to individuals with mixed ancestry, and remnants of this practice continue today in the form of colorism. For "white passing" or "Passe Blanc" individuals who had Black ancestors but appeared to be white, it was often possible to evade the anti-Black racism suffered by the Black community. Whether it was to avoid violence, because of internalized racism, or for the hope of pursuing a life free from hardship, denying one's Black heritage became common for those who could get away with it. Jim Crow officially became constitutional in the United States when the Supreme Court's *Plessy v. Ferguson* (1896) decision declared that segregation was lawful so long as segregated public accommodations were "equal" in nature. This became known as the "separate but equal" doctrine and was ultimately essentially shortened to just "separate" in the minds of most Americans and in the lived experience of most Black Americans.

EVENTS FROM 1861–1900

1861–1865 The Civil War

After years of resentment between the Northern and Southern American states, the issue of slavery and the economic advantages it provided in the South launched the United States into a civil war. The South separated or seceded from the North, which was called the Union, and established a government called the Confederacy. In all, 620,000 people died during the Civil War, and the Union won.

1865–1877 Reconstruction

Reconstruction refers to the laws and policies created following the end of the Civil War. This period aimed to rebuild the South politically and economically while providing aid to formerly enslaved Black people and continued until Rutherford B. Hayes was elected president and dismantled the infrastructure that had been created.

1860

1863 The Emancipation Proclamation

President Abraham Lincoln issued the Emancipation Proclamation during the Civil War to incite political and military instability within the Confederate States. While it marked the beginning of the end for chattel slavery, it applied only to the Confederate States, meaning that those states that had participated in slavery but had not left the Union were not obligated to free enslaved people.

1865 The Thirteenth Amendment

This amendment to the Constitution banned slavery and all involuntary servitude, except in the case of punishment for a crime.

1868 The Fourteenth Amendment

This amendment defined an American citizen as any person born in or "naturalized" in the United States.

1870 The Fifteenth Amendment

The Fifteenth Amendment prohibited governments from denying U.S. citizens the right to vote based on race, color, or past servitude, thus extending voting rights to Black men. It's notable that these new protections did not extend to Native Americans, who were not granted citizenship until 1924 with the passage of the Snyder Act.

1871 Civil Rights Act of 1871

This act was also called the Enforcement Act or the Ku Klux Klan Act. The U.S. Congress passed this legislation to provide accountability for hate groups—namely, the Ku Klux Klan. For example, the law set out to protect Black people from being disenfranchised by hate groups. This act was largely symbolic in nature, because it did little to curtail such hate crimes as lynching which proliferated over the following decades.

1870

1880

1867–1868 Reconstruction Acts

These laws established a series of policies and programs instituted to provide a process for those states that had seceded during the Civil War to reenter the Union. These acts divided the former Confederacy into five districts that were to be governed by military leaders until new state constitutions could be drafted and approved by the U.S. Congress. The acts further allowed males of all races, with the exception of former Confederate leaders, to participate in the creation of these new constitutions, which were required to provide voting rights to all men regardless of race. States were also required to ratify the Fourteenth Amendment in order to be readmitted to the Union.

1875 The Civil Rights Act of 1875

This law set out to protect American citizens from discrimination in public accommodations, such as in restaurants and parks, and guaranteed equal access to public transportation. However, with no practical means of enforcement, this act was largely symbolic.

1877 Rutherford B. Hayes is elected president and ends the Reconstruction period.

1890

1896 *Plessy v. Ferguson*

The U.S. Supreme Court in *Plessy v. Ferguson* issued a decision concerning racial discrimination and segregation on public transportation. This landmark decision held that as long as the segregated facilities were "equal," segregation was constitutional. This decision came to be known as the "separate but equal" doctrine that became the justification for Jim Crow laws across the United States, until the Supreme Court overturned this decision during the landmark cases of the Civil Rights movement.

THE FIRST GREAT MIGRATION

By the turn of the century, survival was on the minds of many Black Americans. In 1900, approximately 90 percent of all Black Americans lived in the South, and life was rife with hardship. Sharecropping and tenant farming had largely replaced slavery. Under the system of sharecropping, tenants would cultivate their landlords' land without pay. In return, tenants and their families were provided with a fraction, or share, of the crops and substandard housing. While chattel slavery had ended four decades earlier, many families were still living in the exact same dwellings as they had when they or their ancestors were enslaved. Tenant farmers were often forced to pay rent for their use of the property, ultimately keeping formerly enslaved people and their descendants in a cycle of crushing debt. The institutional structures that prevented Black people from succeeding continued to evolve, and the Black community was often told to pull themselves up by their bootstraps in a world that deprived them of boots.

Below the Mason–Dixon Line, the glaring threat of racist violence like lynching, coupled with a beetle infestation that decimated what remained of the southern cotton industry, forced many Black Americans to move north in the early 1900s. Jobs were more readily available in northern cities as the outset of World War I created an increased demand for industrial labor. Many companies based in the North promised well-paying industrial jobs and safe havens away from the turbulent South. Also, European immigration dwindled during the war years and Black Americans in the workforce provided a solution to the ensuing labor shortages. In the two years between 1916 and 1918 alone, more than four hundred thousand Black people moved to northern cities. While employment was bountiful, Black men were still underpaid, forcing Black women to seek employment just to keep their families afloat. They took on roles as domestic laborers and service workers decades before the World War II–era image of Rosie the Riveter came to symbolize women joining the workforce. Domestic labor offered higher wages up North than comparable jobs in the South, where workers had to work three weeks to earn the same amount of money that they would have earned in one week in Chicago.

Transportation also played a role in determining where people from the South relocated. Chicago's Black population came primarily from Alabama, Georgia, Louisiana, and Mississippi, correlating to the areas where the Illinois Central Railroad operated. Railroad companies even helped Black southerners resettle up North in order to hire them. The Pennsylvania Railroad employed more than 10,000 Black Americans in 1916 alone; such hiring practices allowed Philadelphia's Black community to grow from 63,000 in 1900 to 134,000 in 1920. Newspapers like *The Chicago Defender* provided resources for Black people living in the South to relocate to Chicago by listing organizations and churches dedicated to helping with resettlement.

Communication between families that had moved north and those who remained in southern communities also created bonds and pipelines for increased migration in later years. Community groups and churches would come to take on a major role in supporting migrants who resettled in northern cities with a focus on literacy and job training programs. To combat the lack of educational institutions, philanthropists and various faith organizations began establishing schools and universities that accepted students of any gender and any race. These schools would later be called Historically Black Colleges or Universties (HBCUs).

A WAY OUT OF NO WAY

Black scholars and entrepreneurs worked to improve conditions against the odds. In 1900, Booker T. Washington, principal at the Tuskegee Institute, a university in Tuskegee, Alabama, founded the National Negro Business League (NNBL) to centralize Black business leaders and accelerate the economic growth of the Black community. While his contributions to education and business were robust, Washington struggled to relate and appeal to the wider Black community. He believed that if Black Americans remained patient and deferential toward the racist status quo, white society would eventually grant them respect and an equal standing, an ideology often called respectability. His stances were embraced by far more white Americans than by those in his own community. To this effect, Washington was able to secure financial investments for his projects like the

NNBL from white capitalists such as Andrew Carnegie. The NNBL allowed entrepreneurs to network, build, and share best practices with their peers. By 1915, the Boston-based organization had six hundred chapters in thirty-four states. It still operates today as the National Business League. To support this effort and to circumvent the legalized discrimination within banking, starting in 1904, minister and businessman Richard H. Boyd joined forces with a group of Black businessmen to create the One Cent Savings Bank in Nashville, Tennessee. Today, it is known as Citizens Bank and is the oldest continuously operating African American–owned bank in the country.

With new opportunities to build wealth, real estate also became a focus of Black investors during the early 1900s. Women, too, were contributing to this

Madam C. J. Walker

Annie Turnbo Malone

landscape of Black entrepreneurship. Two of the most successful moguls of this period included Madam C. J. Walker and Annie Turnbo Malone, who established an entirely Black-owned hair care business, based in St. Louis, Missouri. Maintaining reasonable prices for essential products like pomade and ensuring that these products were accessible through door-to-door sales, Walker and Malone became self-made millionaires. Crucially, they did not hoard these economic resources but distributed them back into the Black community. Both Walker and Malone became philanthropists, funding important literacy and job training programs across the United States.

In 1905, Philip A. Payton's business, the Afro-American Realty Company, was purchasing massive tracts of land in the area of Manhattan known as Harlem.

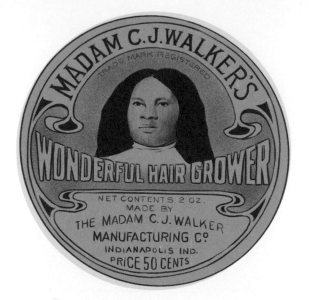

The *New York Times* caught wind of this phenomenon and wrote an article titled "Real Estate Race War Is Started in Manhattan." Payton rallied wealthy Black investors to purchase large tracts of land to house the growing number of Black southerners fleeing north from the brutality of the South. This effort was bolstered by Black churches like the Abyssinian Baptist Church, which since the early 1800s had been developing land in the area. As more Black people moved into Harlem, white neighbors left in what is historically termed "white flight." Over the next decades, this growing community in Harlem would give rise to the Harlem Renaissance.

In 1911, Dr. George Edmund Haynes and Ruth Standish Baldwin founded the National Urban League to provide social support and education to the growing number of Black people in urban areas like New York and St. Louis. To accommodate the massive growth in Chicago's Black community from 30,000 in 1900 to 109,000 in 1920, the Chicago Urban League opened its doors in 1917 to help thousands of newcomers find housing and employment. Despite such robust support systems, the community could not resolve the shortages in housing. Segregated communities, which consisted of dilapidated accommodations, were called ghettos.

In other cities, church organizations like the African Methodist Episcopal Church created charity drives, job training classes, and literacy programs across the United States to support the shifting population and to cultivate community. Literacy among white Americans in 1910 was approximately 95 percent while literacy rates for Black Americans and other Americans of color hovered at 69.5 percent with steady increases over the century.

As Black people continued to move north, politicians and news outlets used fearmongering to take advantage of the racist delusions of white communities, believing that if the public was afraid of the Black community, they could justify increased policing and restrictions against Black people. In East St. Louis, Illinois; Springfield, Illinois; and Chicago, for example, to fuel those feelings of distrust of the Black community, white politicians alleged that Black southerners were being paid to cast multiple votes on election day. Such claims fueled Black voter disenfranchisement, as the white public believed that additional barriers should be created to bar Black people from voting. Unfortunately, charges of this extremely rare kind of election fraud is still a common tactic employed by conservatives to attempt to invalidate progressive change made at the ballot box.

Sensationalism stoked the flames of racism and resentment. Organized backlash and attacks on Black communities were called race riots, although massacre is a more accurate term. In 1908, one such massacre in Springfield, Illinois, was so egregious that it inspired the formation of the National Association for the Advancement of Colored People (NAACP). The NAACP made efforts to establish legal protections, educational opportunities, and social support for Black people across the country. One year after its founding, the organization created its official publication, *The Crisis*, with W. E. B. Du Bois as director of publications and research. Over the ensuing decades, the NAACP would become the foremost civil rights organization supporting landmark civil rights cases, and it continues its transformative work in the current era. Even with the emergence of civil rights organizations dedicated to protecting growing Black communities, violence remained present. Less than a decade after the NAACP was founded, another "race riot" took hold of Illinois in the city of East St. Louis. Even in new cities, safety continued to be elusive for the majority of Black families in America.

Historians widely cite 1916 as the year when the first Great Migration began, with the second wave beginning after the Great Depression. Troublingly, many of these historians also claim that this migration occurred on a voluntary basis instead of being fueled by famine, violence, or genocide. Racial justice scholar Bryan Stevenson is a trailblazer in rewriting this egregious historical erasure. Stevenson's work reveals that throughout the twentieth century, Black Americans were victims of vigilantism fueled by white supremacists. Public executions called lynchings became commonplace. Black men accused of brushing against, speaking to, or even shaking hands with white women would be hung from trees by nooses and lit on fire while they gasped for air. In a display of moral bankruptcy, many people in white communities (including women and children) would flock to these lynchings as if it were a modern-day fireworks display on the Fourth of July.

WORLD WAR I

Despite the racism and challenges they faced in the Jim Crow era, many Black people sought to create spaces for themselves within all parts of American life, including military service, which sat at the heart of American manhood. For African American men, who were often denied the dignity and respect afforded to their white counterparts, undertaking military service became an avenue for individuals to claim their space within the American patriarchy. Black soldiers and soldiers of color were determined to protect democracy and freedom by serving in the war, and in 1917, the U.S. military established segregated infantries for soldiers of color, including the 92nd and 93rd Infantry divisions, where these soldiers served under both Black and white officers years before the U.S. military was desegregated in 1948. These soldiers were not only fighting for their country but were also fighting to be treated equally in their homeland and within their military ranks.

As President Woodrow Wilson shifted America's stance on the Great War from one of neutrality to active involvement, the government became adamant that this war should be fought by white Americans alone. Of the 370,000 Black Americans who had enlisted or had been drafted to serve during World War I, approximately half were assigned to the 92nd and 93rd Infantry groups, while the other half were forced to take up supporting positions as cooks and custodians called messmen. In the Navy, segregation was harshly enforced, limiting Black participation to 10,000 messmen and zero commissioned Black officers.

Despite the blatant racism within the military, Black Americans served bravely for their country; in order to see combat, however, they had to enlist in foreign allied armies. One distinguished group within the 92nd Infantry included the 369th Infantry Regiment—better known as the Harlem Hellfighters—who were forced to join ranks with the French military in order to fight for their own country, America. In 1918, the Harlem Hellfighters became the first Black and Puerto Rican soldiers to see combat during World War I and became the first Allied unit to cross the Rhine River in Germany. In total, these soldiers served for 191 days, the longest duration of service of any American unit during World War I, and they suffered the greatest sacrifice, with 1,500 lives lost as casualties of war. For their efforts, the French military awarded more than 170 medals to individual soldiers and awarded the high honor of the Croix de Guerre to the entire Harlem Hellfighters unit.

Meanwhile, most Americans failed to acknowledge the feats of this elite group because of racism; in fact, bigoted white American soldiers like Colonel J. L. A. Linard were even determined to export their racism abroad. Linard sent an infamous memo chastising French officers for treating their Black counterparts with respect and humanity. He demanded that the French subject American soldiers of color to Jim Crow conditions, meaning that there could be no handshakes between people of different races, "Whites Only" signage needed to be posted on their bases, and curfews imposed for Black soldiers akin to the sundown towns of many American cities. In response, the French released a statement on the inherent value of all men and continued to treat Black soldiers with respect.

The open displays of bigotry from white American troops eventually came to light when W. E. B. Du Bois published the Linard memo in *The Crisis* in 1919, following the end of World War I. Importantly, despite the eventual desegregation of the American military, soldiers of color who served in World War II, the Korean War, and the Vietnam War were subjected to much of the same unfair treatment endured by the Hellfighters.

With one world war under its belt, legislation in the United States pointed toward an attempt at social control. Jim Crow policies continued to press forward in many state legislatures and dictated nearly every aspect of life for Black Americans. In addition to determining the hours during which Black people were allowed to be seen in public, these same policies determined who was allowed to use which restrooms, water fountains, public areas, and more. During this same period, America was jailing reproductive health advocates such as Jewish American activist Emma Goldman for educating communities about birth control, and in 1919 the U.S. Congress passed the Eighteenth Amendment, which prohibited the sale and consumption of alcohol across the United States. While it seemed that America was about to enjoy a new level of economic prosperity in the next decade, a vice grip of governmental control would leave Black people, people of color, and women of all races behind.

W. E. B. Du Bois

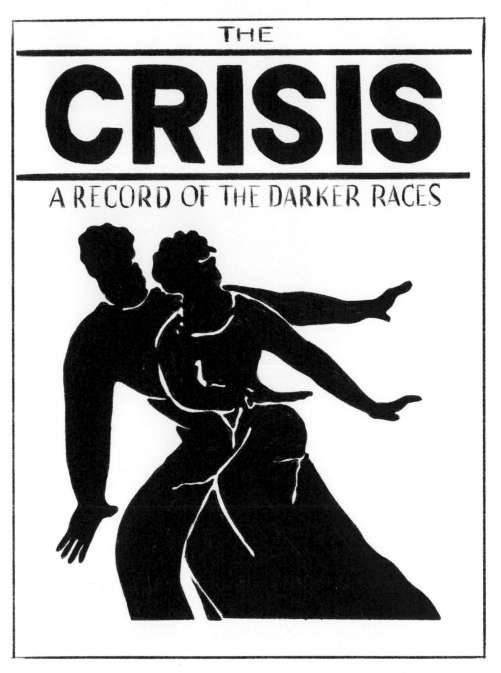

Cover of *The Crisis*, March 1933

BEAUTIFUL—
AND UGLY, TOO

1920—1929

AS VETERANS RETURNED FROM THE GREAT WAR, Black Americans and Native Americans were prevented from fully participating in the affairs of government. On paper, Black people possessed the right to vote; however, myriad barriers like poll taxes, vigilantism, and literacy tests prevented the majority of the Black community from exercising that right. Poll taxes meant that only people with the requisite finances could vote because the fee did not differ based on an individual's income, thus placing voting out of reach for many. Racist vigilantism in the form of lynching meant that voting could place a Black person and their family in harm's way if they were even seen at the polling place. Literacy tests, which were essentially a series of trick questions, meant that only those with a significant amount of patience, mental fortitude, and luck could participate in the electoral process. If you managed to ace the "test," you were still left to the subjective grading scale of the person reviewing your exam. Because literacy tests were disproportionately distributed to Black people, they were little more than a tool of white supremacy to keep Black people disenfranchised. Similarly, grandfather clauses instituted at the local and state levels disproportionately excluded Black people from voting, because these clauses waived the above barriers for folks whose grandfathers were previously registered to vote. At a time when most Black folks' grandparents had been enslaved, this was an example of institutionalized racism. Native American individuals did not obtain full U.S. citizenship until the passage of the Snyder Act in 1924, despite having had a presence in America that preceded that of the white people who had colonized and stolen their land. Unable to participate in government, people of color grew frustrated and disillusioned with the way their country was treating them.

Following the end of World War I in 1918, Congress took action to curtail the number of European and Asian immigrants entering the United States. The rising influence of white supremacist hate groups like the Ku Klux Klan (KKK) contributed to the increasingly narrow view of who could be an American. The Immigration Act of 1924 shut down the immigration of people from Asia, while setting quotas or limits for the number of immigration documents granted to people from European countries. The wave of restrictive policies even resulted in the closure of Ellis Island in 1924. Faced with the decision of employing Black people or failing to meet production goals, most industry leaders opened their assembly lines to Black people. This increased need also softened the immigration restrictions that applied to immigrants from the Caribbean and from South and Central America. In 1910, approximately 600 out of the 100,000 American automotive factory workers in the United States were Black. But by 1929, the number of Black automotive workers boomed to approximately 25,000. Once wary of employing Black people, the Ford Motor Company employed the greatest number of Black people in the state of Michigan: 15,000 by the end of the 1920s. The promise of these new job opportunities drew waves of Black newcomers from the South and the Caribbean to new homes in the North during the 1920s.

SURVIVAL

In 1929, Texas blues singer Blind Lemon Jefferson sang about the violent realities faced by the Black community in his song "Hangman's Blues." The song described the constant threat of lynching that Black people faced during what historians call the nadir (the lowest point) of American race relations. Lynching extinguished the lives of thousands of Black men, women, and children. While most lynchings took place in the South, anti-Black violence could erupt anywhere—just as it had in Illinois during the previous decade. Lynchings were hate crimes and for the most part took place outside of the law. Many lynchings included beatings, castration, rape, and any other form of violence that one human being could inflict on another.

For those who carried out lynchings or participated in them by being onlookers, the act of violence was seen as vigilante justice or community law enforcement against "animalistic" and "dangerous" Black people and immigrants. During slavery, slaveholders often publicly beat any enslaved person who was caught defying the status quo, and in a similar way, lynchings became a mechanism to traumatize, intimidate, and dehumanize an entire community. Many lynchings were even photographed and displayed on postcards. These images often depicted the charred body of a Black person hanging from a tree branch with a rope formed into a noose around their neck, while a sea of white-faced onlookers smiled for the camera.

With few protections, the type of violence suffered by the Black community included harm not only to their bodies but also to their livelihoods, families, and futures. In 1921, a nationally renowned enclave of Black wealth, often called Black Wall Street, became the site of the Tulsa Massacre. As Black businesspeople were systematically prevented from engaging in Wall Street affairs under a system of segregation, Black Wall Street, which was home to Black-owned and -operated businesses, was swiftly becoming the epicenter of Black industrial growth and economic prosperity in the years that followed World War I. The families that lived in the Greenwood District of Tulsa, Oklahoma, were starting to lay the groundwork for generational wealth within the Black community. The domestic terrorism that ensued, following an alleged incident involving a Black teenage boy and white teenage girl, caused a powder keg of racism and hatred to explode on the night of May 30, 1921, ultimately extinguishing the economic growth that the Black community in Tulsa had achieved. On that evening, thousands of white men and women burned the homes and businesses of the Black residents in the Greenwood District. The estimate for the number of Black people killed ranged from the official count of sixty to the community's count of three hundred. Over ten thousand Black people were left homeless, and the property losses and damage totaled $31 million when adjusted for today's inflation. One year later, the KKK marched through the streets of Greenwood in full regalia to further intimidate the survivors of that horrific event. It was not until eight decades later, in 2001, that an official inquiry was pursued to determine the facts about the Tulsa Massacre.

Rebuilding and healing were left to the now-displaced Black community, while the local government attempted to thwart any rebuilding attempts. The American Red Cross assisted where the U.S. government refused, because it was clear that America had no interest in protecting or adequately resourcing Black people. While the Tulsa Massacre demonstrated an extreme consequence of racism, the sentiments that had sparked the violence were not rare. A vast majority of white Americans felt threatened by any advancement made by Black people.

Ella Fitzgerald

THE BLACK RENAISSANCE

As new Black neighbors made their homes in northern cities to secure jobs and seize new opportunities, they brought their traditions and experiences along with them. In the 1920s, the predominantly Black area of Manhattan called Harlem became a home to the vibrant artistic, cultural, and social movement known as the Harlem Renaissance, and across the country, similar movements were taking root. Within just two decades, Harlem's Black population grew from just under twenty-five thousand in 1910 to over two hundred thousand by 1930.

During this era, lasting changes were made to the landscape of American music, literature, and culture. Jazz music, which had emerged in New Orleans following the Civil War, gained new heights of popularity during the 1920s and gave rise to myriad musical artists. Above Manhattan's Central Park, Harlem nightclubs introduced blues from St. Louis and Memphis and jazz from New Orleans to a new mostly white audience. In an era where Black people and white people lived largely separate lives, music and culture became the realm where a view into the lives of America's darker-hued citizens could be gleaned. The Cotton Club and the Sugar Cane Club popularized Black artists like bisexual blues singer Bessie Smith and improvisational jazz icon Ella Fitzgerald. Louis Armstrong toured across the United States in jazz clubs from New Orleans to New York, and internationally renowned musician Duke Ellington made history in the musical genre of jazz, even as he was defining it. In Harlem clubs, the

Alain Locke

performers were vibrant, illegal alcohol was abundant, and audiences consisting of white New Yorkers and visiting Europeans eagerly indulged in the cultural rebirth. While these clubs capitalized on the new interest in Black artists, most establishments allowed only white customers. This meant that while Bessie Smith, Duke Ellington, Louis Armstrong, and Ella Fitzgerald were allowed to perform, their families and friends were not welcome. Fortunately, Ed Smalls broke away from this racist exploitation when he opened a jazz club named Smalls Paradise in 1925. In addition to being Black owned, Smalls Paradise was racially integrated, meaning that the Black people who had created the Harlem Renaissance were now able to enjoy its fruits.

Philosopher and educator Alain Locke spearheaded this movement and helped inspire a new generation of Black artists, intellectuals, and political leaders with his foundational 1925 work *The New Negro*, which advocated for a new way of seeing Black identity within the context of American life. Locke wrote that the new Black community "lays aside the status of beneficiary and ward for that of a collaborator and participant in American civilization." This call to recognize Black individuality and humanity spoke to many young people who were similarly eager to reject the prejudices and second-class status thrust upon them by American institutions. The Harlem Renaissance, also called the New Negro movement after Locke's philosophy and text, was the seemingly perfect combination of timing, opportunity, and creativity. The discovery of King Tutankhamen's tomb in Egypt in 1921 sparked an international obsession with African culture. And as the need for increased labor sparked movement to cities following World War I, Black people from countless backgrounds began working and collaborating in new ways. Harlem was a central location because it had one of the largest Black communities at the time. These forces all coalesced into a rebirth and forged a new appreciation for Black contributions to art, literature, culture, and music.

Importantly, this new movement also took steps to banish homophobia and sexism, with social clubs, theater troupes, and publications making space and providing resources to the emerging talents of every gender and sexual orientation. Gladys Bentley, a prominent figure during this time, was a performer and an outspoken Black lesbian who did not dress according to traditional gender expectations. She wore exquisite three-piece suits and top hats in her performances,

<< Louis Armstrong and Duke Ellington

A. Philip Randolph

where she was known to sing salacious lyrics and openly flirt with women in the audience. Ma Rainey, also known as the Mother of the Blues, is also remembered as a bisexual woman, who declared in one of her songs, "Prove It on Me Blues" (1928), "I went out last night with a crowd of my friends, It must've been women, 'cause I don't like no men." It is difficult to discern how Bentley and Rainey may have identified, because being part of the LGBTQ community and coming out was very different then from what it is today. During the rise of the Harlem Renaissance, queer or LGBTQ identity was just another element of the movement that redefined the expectations thrust upon Black people in white society.

From 1926 to 1930, the Harmon Foundation, which had been established by philanthropist and real estate developer William E. Harmon, established the appropriately named William E. Harmon Foundation Award for Distinguished Achievement Among Negroes that recognized distinguished achievement among Black people across eight fields, including race relations, fine arts, literature, education, industry, religious service, science, and music. Crucially, this recognition provided not only increased visibility but also financial awards, serving a purpose similar to what the patrons of the arts had done during the Italian Renaissance in the 1300s. With access to such funding and little obligation to those who had provided the resources, artists and scholars were able to cultivate their crafts on a new level. Publications like A. Philip Randolph's *The Messenger*, the National Urban League's *Opportunity*, and the National Association for the Advancement of Colored People's (NAACP's) *The Crisis* provided unprecedented space for

Zora Neale Hurston

emerging talents like Claude McKay and James Weldon Johnson to express themselves and reach new audiences.

Leaders of the Harlem Renaissance came from across the country through the Great Migration and contributed to the culture that allowed for creative self-expression. Zora Neale Hurston, who was born in Alabama and raised in Florida, found a home and chosen family among luminaries of the Harlem Renaissance. Before arriving in New York, Hurston published stories in *Opportunity* and quickly established herself as a skilled storyteller. Her work earned her a place at the *Opportunity* awards dinner in Harlem in May 1925, where the young new-comer earned two awards for her drama *Color Struck* and short story "Spunk." Seemingly overnight, Hurston was in the company of esteemed intellectuals like

Richard B. Nugent

Langston Huhges

openly gay artist Richard B. Nugent and prolific poet Langston Hughes. Like Hurston, Nugent's and Hughes's poetry first appeared in the Black publications that facilitated the rise of new artists—Nugent submitted his poem "Shadow" to *Opportunity* at the urging of Hughes. The poem interrogated the sudden visibility that he and his contemporaries were experiencing due to the Harlem Renaissance. Simultaneously, Hughes published poems about the beauty and complexity of the Black community. In his 1926 essay *Negro Artist and the Racial Mountain*, Hughes praised the contributions of his contemporaries and criticized their missteps, ultimately capturing the spirit of the Harlem Renaissance: "We younger Negro artists who create now intend to express our individual

Cover of *Fire!!*, 1926

dark-skinned selves without fear or shame. If white people are pleased, we are glad. If they are not, it doesn't matter. We know we are beautiful. And ugly too."

The exploration of the themes of the New Negro movement included the creation of an experimental publication called *Fire!!*, which Hughes and Nugent cofounded in 1926. Alongside influential literary figures like Hurston, Countee Cullen, and Gwendolyn Bennett, *Fire!!*, which was "devoted to younger Negro artists," explored sexuality, colorism, privilege, feminism, and more. Key contributors to the magazine, including Nugent, were openly part of the LGBTQ community making *Fire!!* perhaps the first Black- and LGBTQ- created publication in the United States. While initially intended to be a series, the magazine was limited to only one issue, because the headquarters where *Fire!!* was produced burned down in an ironic twist of fate.

Poet Lucy Ariel Williams Holloway wrote about the experience of Black southerners who headed north for improved opportunities in *Opportunity* in 1926. Although she had been born in Brooklyn, her poem "Northboun'" (excerpt below) used the southern vernacular that many Black newcomers brought with them as they moved to new cities. Her poem captured the common perspective that inspired Black Americans to move North.

Huh! de wurl' ain't flat,	Huh! the world ain't flat,
An' de wurl' ain't roun',	And the world ain't round,
Jes' one long strip	Just one long strip
Hangin' up an' down.	Hanging up and down.
Since Norf is up,	Since North is up,
An' Souf is down,	And South is down,
An' Hebben is up,	And Heaven is up,
I'm upward boun'.	I'm upward bound.

The Black experience had never been monolithic, and the social, cultural, and political exploration that took place during the Harlem Renaissance allowed Black people to define themselves in new ways. Leaders with different life experiences developed differing approaches toward navigating Black identity within the United States. Scholars like W. E. B. Du Bois used the written and spoken word to build upon the foundations laid by Ida B. Wells and Frederick Douglass in order to uplift and accelerate change for the Black community. Over the span of his prolific writing career, Du Bois penned *The Souls of Black Folk* (1903), *The Negro* (1915), and *Black Reconstruction in America* (1935), which alongside works by Locke, helped redefine and explore Black identity in the United States. Du Bois, a cofounder of the NAACP, became editor of the organization's publication, *The Crisis*, which provided opportunities for emerging Black writers, poets, and playwrights to gain prominence. *The Crisis*, which was in wide distribution during the 1920s, also served to include Black people who may not have been otherwise able to engage with the Harlem Renaissance.

The literature and political ideology that emerged during this period helped define a new chapter of Black identity. One of those ideologies included Garveyism, named for its originator, Jamaican political leader Marcus Garvey. Garveyism urges the complete self-reliance of Black people globally, including military, economic, and political independence. While America had decided that it was entirely constitutional to separate Black people from white people in every realm of life, the notion of Black independence alarmed the U.S. government. Garvey's organization, the Universal Negro Improvement Association (UNIA), was viewed as militant and radical, terms that would come to define groups that presented a threat to the white supremacist status quo. America feared that the growing number of disillusioned World War I veterans—especially Black soldiers who had risked their lives for a country that did not value them—would gravitate to the ideals of Garveyism. For many, a new philosophy was needed, and Garveyism became the answer.

An increasingly wary government took steps to infiltrate Garvey's organization, and under J. Edgar Hoover, the Federal Bureau of Investigation (FBI) hired its first full-time Black agent, James Wormley Jones, in 1919. Jones was charged with gathering information to use against Garvey—similar tactics would later be used to disrupt Black organizations that formed during the Civil Rights movement. Garvey reinvigorated the Back to Africa movement, which encouraged people of African descent to return to the lands from which their ancestors had been stolen. Disillusioned Black people who had relocated to the North and returning veterans found hope in the notion of returning to their ancestral homes. While Garvey's vision of a wholly independent Black community remained elusive in the United States, his work represented a new era of political ideology for Black people globally. His legacy informed the decolonization movement in Africa and the work of the Black Panthers and other civil rights organizations in later years.

Marcus Garvey

I, TOO, AM AMERICA

1930–1939

THE 1920S ENDED WITH THE ECONOMIC DEVASTATION of the stock market crash of 1929. In most cities, both in the North and in the South, the unemployment rate for Black people was higher than that of their white counterparts. As a result of the economic collapse, the first wave of the Great Migration, which lasted from 1910 until 1930, drew to a close. Black families struggled to secure employment and support, because social and job programs tended to give priority to white people. Soup kitchens, shelters, and most other public aid organizations were segregated. President Herbert Hoover's administration demonstrated a steadfast refusal to directly intervene. Under Hoover, the U.S. government chose to allow the free market economy to sort out the chaos of the Great Depression rather than using

Mary McLeod Bethune

government spending to ease the rippling effects of the collapse. By the 1932 election, Americans were desperate for change, and when Franklin Delano Roosevelt (FDR) ran for president in 1933, he presented an opportunity for a shift in policy.

After FDR was elected, he acted on campaign promises to aid suffering families, and he swiftly enacted programs dedicated to alleviating the crushing poverty created by the Great Depression. In 1935, Black American education advocate Mary McLeod Bethune became an influential advisor to FDR, and she formed a friendship with First Lady Eleanor Roosevelt. Bethune's widely publicized friendship with Eleanor Roosevelt coincided with the Black community's increased support of FDR. Eventually, historical voting patterns by Black people shifted from overwhelmingly Republican to majority Democrat. In fact, the historical association between Black people and the Democratic Party began during the 1936 election. Bethune would go on to found and become the director of the National Youth Administration's Office of Negro Affairs during Roosevelt's second term in office. Roosevelt promised that under his presidency, America would be back to work, and he used a series of economic stimulus programs called the New Deal to do so. The New Deal ultimately broadened the wealth gap between Black and white Americans by prioritizing white participants, allowing lower pay for Black workers, and segregating the programs. The administration's attempts to deliver on promises made to all of America stopped short of including the Black community and Americans of color.

An Olympic gold medalist named Jesse Owens exemplified America's struggle to maintain a policy of white supremacy. For Black people, Owens would become a national hero while also defying the myth of white superiority. He was born in 1913 in Oakville, Alabama, to sharecropper parents with extremely limited opportunity for advancement. Like thousands of other Black people seeking better opportunities, Owens and his family moved north to Cleveland, Ohio, in the early 1920s. In Cleveland, he was able to get part-time jobs and contribute to his family's income, attend school, and make a name for himself as a high school track and field athlete. Owens continued to pursue his career in track and field, and in 1935, he qualified for the 1936 Berlin Summer Olympics. Adolf Hitler, who was the ruler of Nazi Germany at the time, represented a deeply racist, anti-Semitic, and fascist regime that prompted the National Association for the Advancement of Colored

People (NAACP) and other civil rights organizations to push for a complete boycott of the Berlin Olympics. Participation in the Games by Black Olympians directly threatened the nations of Aryan supremacy espoused by Hitler's regime. Owens won four Olympic gold medals, and his Black teammate, Cornelius Johnson, also won a gold. In an attempt to highlight the racism of Hitler's regime, an American newspaper fabricated a story that alleged that Johnson and Owens had been snubbed by Hitler. But in reality, the political leader who snubbed Owens and Johnson was someone far closer to home: FDR refused to meet with or congratulate the Black Olympians. Owens would later recall, "Although I wasn't invited to shake hands with Hitler, I wasn't invited to the White House to shake hands with the President either." Still, American media ran with the fabricated story that allowed the United States to place itself on the moral high ground despite the grim and racist reality of American daily life. It was an all-too-familiar irony faced by Black America.

As the Great Depression devastated workers in urban cities, agricultural workers in the Midwest and South faced a severe drought in 1931 that caused crops to wither away. Farmers had nothing to sell in order to generate much-needed income, and the dust storms that ravaged the parched, naked landscape—an area of the United States that became known as the Dust Bowl—defined this era from 1930 until 1936. By 1934, an area in America's heartland the size of Iowa that had previously been used for farming lay barren. Unable to work the soil or turn a profit, Midwestern farmers and agricultural workers moved westward to pursue better opportunities.

While Black people were among those affected and those who relocated, during this time period they have been largely erased by mainstream history. Simultaneously, the hardships of white families during this time have been romanticized and chronicled at length by acclaimed authors and documentarians like John Steinbeck and Ken Burns, who completely failed to mention Black Americans during this time at all. Some historians claim that the movement of 2.5 million people from the Midwest to the West during the Dust Bowl era was the largest internal migration in American history. But this is an obviously whitewashed narrative that overlooks the fact that six million Black people migrated internally across the United States during the first and second Great Migrations

Jesse Owens

Mary McLeod Bethune and Eleanor Roosevelt

from 1910 to 1979. During the first wave of the Great Migration, from 1910 to 1930, 1.5 million individuals left the rural South for urban cities in the North like New York, St. Louis, Detroit, and Chicago. Sympathy for the white families fleeing the Dust Bowl still runs deep in America's mainstream historical narrative, but this same sympathy is not generally extended to the legions of Black people fleeing the South, due to issues such as domestic terrorism during the Great Migration.

SAME OLD NEW DEAL

After Americans had suffered through a presidential administration that refused to directly intervene in the economic collapse caused by the stock market crash of 1929, FDR, the newly elected president, was welcomed with open arms by a nation to whom he had promised a new deal. The New Deal was a series of spending programs aimed to revitalize the struggling U.S. economy. FDR pledged that Americans would be headed back to work despite the staggering unemployment numbers. To accomplish this, FDR established the Civilian Conservation Corps (CCC) in 1933. On its face, the CCC appeared to be an amazing opportunity for economic and educational betterment for the young men who were able to participate. Every month, the CCC members would earn $30 (approximately $587 in today's money) for working to build roads, plant trees, and erect campsites in the national parks. Of the $30, $25 was to be sent home to provide for their families. While a Black congressman from Illinois named Oscar De Priest successfully advocated for the inclusion of nondiscrimination language in the law that established the CCC, the U.S. government (which still determined segregation to be constitutional) allowed states to outright refuse to include Black workers. As time went on, the CCC eventually created segregated programs for Black people and Native Americans. But of the nearly 3.5 million CCC enrollees from 1933 to 1941, only 7 percent were Black and only 2 percent were Native American. Black enrollment was limited to 10 percent of the total enrollees each year to reflect the total population of Black people within the United States. But this quota policy did not address the more dire circumstances faced by Black people—unequal access to education, voting rights, and outright racism—and instead prevented Black people from competing on an equal playing field.

In rural areas, a New Deal program called the Agricultural Adjustment Act (1933) attempted to incentivize farmers to plant fewer crops in order to stabilize the prices of agricultural products. As an ally during World War I, America had enlisted its farmers to begin growing crops to export to European countries, where the countryside had been transformed into trench-marked battlefields. After the war, as Europe stopped relying on imported goods and began raising its own crops and produce, American farmers did not adjust their practices to account for this decreased need, and they began to grow more crops than they could sell, creating what is called a surplus. Stabilizing the agricultural economy was one of FDR's first actions as president. Under the 1933 Agricultural Adjustment Act, farmers were financially compensated for decreasing the acreage in use on their farms. The theory behind this program was that if the surplus could be eliminated, the prices of produce would stabilize, providing a long-term economic benefit. It was the landowners, who were predominantly white, who were the benefactors of this government spending program, because they could save or even make money if they used less land, and not the Black agricultural workers who cultivated the land. At a time when 40 percent of Black people worked as sharecroppers, the New Deal program only exacerbated the wealth divide along racial lines, as Black sharecroppers were fired.

While they may have been well intentioned, many of FDR's New Deal programs worsened the stark racial inequities within the land of the free. In Ira Katznelson's text on the subject, *When Affirmative Action Was White*, he notes that approximately 65 percent of Black people were prevented from accessing the social welfare programs created to aid the elderly, poor, and unemployed due to racial quotas and because the Social Security Act did not apply to career fields historically held by Black people. In 1944, following the end of World War II, the G.I. Bill would similarly escalate economic disparities between veterans of color and their white counterparts.

COMMUNITY ORGANIZING

While the New Deal ostensibly helped the American economy bounce back from the Great Depression, it badly aggravated the disparities between Black and white Americans. During this time, many Black Americans continued to establish organizations and institutions to intervene where the government had failed. Many faith organizations helped the Black community endure the pervasive impact of America's anti-Black racism, with two Islamic religious organizations gaining prominence during this time: the Moorish Science Temple of America and the Nation of Islam, founded in 1913 and 1930, respectively. While wholly distinct, these two organizations helped many Black Americans orient themselves amid the changing landscape of the United States during the Great Migration.

For people with labor-intensive agricultural jobs, the economic decline of the Great Depression did not come as a surprise. People in rural areas witnessed a decline in prosperity that came well before the crash of the stock market. Since 1910, the number of Black sharecroppers had steadily decreased as folks found better opportunities or were fired as more farms became mechanized. The remaining sharecroppers formed labor unions to retain the little economic control they possessed. The Southern Tenant Farmers Union (STFU) was formed in Arkansas in 1934 and consisted of Black and white Americans. Labor organizing was not new to the South, although the STFU became a target of violence and vigilantism by hate groups throughout the 1930s, because it united farmers across race. Despite the threats and violence, the union boasted membership in Arkansas, Missouri, Oklahoma, Tennessee, and Texas just two years after its founding. The STFU made great strides in laying the groundwork of activist and organizer networks, but due to the violence suffered by members who dared to challenge the status quo and because of an increased focus on industrial jobs in the 1940s, it eventually ceased operation.

Labor organizing and workers unions enjoyed further protections under the National Labor Relations Act (or Wagner Act), which FDR signed on July 5, 1935. The Wagner Act allowed workers to unionize and collectively bargain with employers, but the act did not protect agricultural or domestic workers, who were mostly Black.

An earlier labor union, the Brotherhood of Sleeping Car Porters, became the first labor union for Black Americans in 1925. That year, laborers joined forces with civil rights leader A. Philip Randolph, who helped the porters become an official union, ensuring that thousands of Black workers secured improved conditions and increased pay. During the 1930s, when the majority of Americans were facing financial ruin and unemployment, the porters enjoyed job security, thanks to the luxury railcar services utilized by some of the most privileged Americans. The first Pullman porters were freedmen hired by George Pullman to provide wealthy white train travelers with personal servants, a notion that reeked of the recently abolished institution of slavery. While highly respected within their own communities because of steady and relatively high-paying jobs, porters were forced to suffer indignities like being asked to sing and dance on command by America's white elite. During slavery, enslaved people were forced to answer to the name of their owner, effectively erasing their individual identity. This custom continued as Black porters were forced to respond to the name "George" after George Pullman, their employer. Despite these humiliations, porters are remembered for ushering in a new echelon of financial security for working class Black Americans during a time when the only constant was uncertainty. Pullman porters were able to send their children to college and work toward better economic and educational futures for their families and their communities. They are remembered for feats in labor organizing and for their role in helping to establish the Black middle class.

A Pullman Porter >>

Pullman porters were able to have larger-than-average families because of a steady income.

LIBERTY AND JUSTICE FOR ALL?

1940–1949

THE SECOND WAVE OF THE GREAT MIGRATION TOOK OFF DURING THE 1940S; this movement would be much larger, giving rise to new civil rights across the country. From 1940 to 1979, more than 5 million Black people would migrate across the United States, with 1.5 million Black people leaving the rural South in the 1940s alone. As this migration took place, local and national organizations were working to house and protect growing Black communities. In 1940, the National Association for the Advancement of Colored People (NAACP) established the Legal Defense Fund in New York City, which provided much-needed resources to dismantle segregation and discrimination by taking the fight against racism to the courts through legal action. Massive government defense spending created new centers of industry along the West Coast. Millions of Americans who had spent the previous decade unemployed due to the Great Depression were now able to get back to work. America had become the great arsenal of democracy under its longest-serving president, Franklin Delano Roosevelt (FDR). The United States and its citizens would be the suppliers of everything from bullets to tanks for Allied forces fighting in World War II.

As the defense industry expanded, civil rights leaders pressured FDR to expand access to these stable and well-paying jobs to Black people. After being ignored by the president, civil rights organizers Bayard Rustin and A. Philip Randolph began to organize a mass demonstration for July 1, 1941, in protest of the segregated defense industry. When faced with this additional pressure of a forthcoming protest, FDR signed Executive Order 8802 on June 25, 1941, which prohibited ethnic and racial discrimination within the nation's defense industries. FDR declared that all Americans, regardless of race or gender, were needed to bolster the number of hands on assembly lines. While the 1941 march was canceled, Rustin would revive this type of political pressure years later alongside Dr. Martin Luther King Jr. in 1963. As in World War I, Black soldiers were prevented from fully participating in the military, but Black people were reluctantly embraced as laborers on the assembly lines tasked with building up America's arsenal. Still, hate persisted, as some white workers preferred to go on strike in response to the hiring and promotion of Black workers rather than work alongside them.

In rural areas, where the majority of Black Americans still lived following the Great Depression, the dismal economy of the 1930s had not improved by the 1940s. Many Black families chose to relocate at the outset of World War II in pursuit of the American dream, as recruiters from industrial companies in urban areas promised opportunity and gainful employment. America at war meant America at work. With the establishment of the Fair Employment Practice Committee by Executive Order 8802, Black people and people of color were able to access the stability of wartime prosperity. Black people flocked to manufacturing cities like Detroit, Baltimore, and Chicago, where families that had left the South during the first Great Migration were already established.

Bayard Rustin

In 1941, the Japanese attack on Pearl Harbor thrust Americans out of isolationism and into the fray of World War II, immediately igniting a patriotic fervor among Americans from all walks of life. Still, while historians claim that a common enemy abroad united Americans in an unprecedented manner, the historical record reveals that people of color in the United States continued to endure a precarious existence. African American soldiers were forced to serve in segregated Black units in menial, noncombat positions or serve in battalions abroad just as they had in World War I. On the home front, Black people faced violence from hate groups enraged by the population swell of Black families in previously white-dominated cities.

Mass hysteria following the bombing of Pearl Harbor resulted in one of the most overt human rights abuses perpetuated by the American government: in February 1942, FDR signed Executive Order 9066, which condemned immigrants from Japan and American citizens of Japanese ancestry to internment camps across the United States. Tens of thousands of people of Japanese descent were forced to sell their belongings and property at a loss or abandon it altogether to comply with this fascist mandate. As my grandmother Verna Jean recalled, "One day our friends were sitting in class with us, and the next day we were surrounded by empty seats." Under the system of segregation, Japanese students and other students of color attended school with Black students. Thousands of Japanese people were forced into internment camps with no distinction made between *issei* (immigrants) and citizens who were *nisei* (second generation). In some cases, *sansei* (third generation Japanese people) were exempt from the relocation program. Still, many soldiers of Black and Japanese ancestry enlisted to protect the country they called home. Segregation ruled the lives of Black people, people of color, and Jewish Americans during the years of World War II and beyond. Like the soldiers of color who had served in World War I, these heroes were fighting not just for their country's freedom but also for the personal freedoms that institutional racism denied to them and their families.

By the end of the 1940s, the rift between Americans of color and their white counterparts had deepened yet again. The Servicemen's Readjustment Act (1944), better known as the G.I. Bill, afforded housing, work, and education to returning veterans. Still, with little infrastructure to protect against racism, many Black soldiers and soldiers of color were unable to access the wealth that defined the postwar country. Women who had joined the workforce were replaced with returning men, because the labor shortage caused by the war had ended. Although the postwar prosperity of the late 1940s ushered a majority of America into new wealth, it also left legions of Americans behind.

MILITARY SERVICE

America was shaken by the Japanese military attack at Pearl Harbor on December 7, 1941. One Black American man, Doris Miller, became a hero for his actions to save his comrades in the midst of an attack that claimed the lives of 2,403 American servicemen and civilians. Like many Black people who had joined the military, Miller was born in the South but had relocated to the West when he enlisted in 1939. He served as a cook or "messman" on the USS *West Virginia* at Pearl Harbor. At 7:57 a.m. on the morning of the fatal attack, Miller was busy collecting laundry, when blaring battle sirens prompted him to report for duty. Despite not having been trained in using any weaponry, he successfully took over a machine gun and fired at Japanese military planes until he was forced to abandon ship. The U.S. military was predictably reluctant to praise an African American soldier even for such heroic acts, but after campaigning from the NAACP and press coverage from Black publications like the *Pittsburgh Courier*, Miller became the first Black American to receive the Navy Cross for his valiant actions during the attack. Miller's willingness to risk life and limb to protect his country was echoed by thousands of Black people who enlisted in the days following December 7, 1941. Miller did not survive the war; he was killed in action in 1943, but his legacy reflects the countless Black people who have been written out of American history. Black newspapers ran headlines, reading: "Mr. President, count on us," which demonstrated a steadfast willingness to serve. Boxer Joe Louis even promised prize money from his next two fights to go to the Army and Navy relief funds. However, despite the fierce patriotism of Black Americans, the majority of Black soldiers were relegated to auxiliary positions supporting white soldiers. The more than one million Black women and men who served during World War II did so despite racism and mandated segregation, carving out a space for themselves and their communities in the larger story of American history.

Doris Miller

At the outset of World War II, all types of military service were open to white soldiers, while Black soldiers were denied equal access to training and positions. White military leaders and government officials overwhelmingly believed that Black people were intellectually and physically inferior, and this attitude was reinforced throughout society. In 1925, the U.S. Army War College issued a post–World War I memorandum titled "The Use of Negro Manpower in War" that presented pseudoscience alleging that Black pilots were unable to match the prowess of white pilots and encouraged the continued segregation of the military. By 1939, little had changed with regard to this kind of thinking in the military. But as American institutions clung to white supremacy, Black civil rights organizations were working to pry open the hands that held onto it. In 1939, the NAACP began a legal battle to integrate the military. Alongside the legal efforts, Black publications like the *Chicago Defender* and the *Pittsburgh Courier* educated the public about the injustice of military segregation. By the time America got involved in World War II, the NAACP's efforts had culminated in the establishment of a segregated Air Corps and the creation of a training program at the Tuskegee Institute in Alabama in July 1941.

Just six months after the establishment of the training program at the Tuskegee Institute, America was officially at war. At that time, one of the three major units established by this program, the 99th Pursuit Squadron, had 429 enlisted Black men and 47 white officers. Less than a year later, there were approximately 3,000 personnel stationed at the Tuskegee Army Air Field. Later, Black soldiers were ordered to report to Captain Benjamin O. Davis Jr., one of only two Black army captains serving in the United States. Called the Tuskegee Airmen after the training location, these distinguished men were the first Black military aviators in American history, and they made an indelible mark on society. From 1940 to 1946, the Tuskegee program trained 996 pilots; 445 of those pilots were deployed overseas. In total, the Tuskegee Airmen were involved in 15,000 combat runs, winning 150 Distinguished Flying Crosses, 744 Air Medals, 8 Purple Hearts, and 14 Bronze Stars. These airmen made grave sacrifices—66 pilots were killed in action and 32 were captured as prisoners of war.

In large part because of the successes of the training unit, the Tuskegee Airmen made the U.S. government reconsider its previously held biases against Black soldiers and Black pilots in particular. The Tuskegee Airmen came from the same cities that Black Americans had moved to during the first wave of the Great Migration, including Chicago, Detroit, New York, and Philadelphia. While serving abroad in places like Sicily, North Africa, and Italy, the soldiers in the Tuskegee units were treated as relative equals to their European and African counterparts—a similar experience to that of the Harlem Hellfighters during World War I. Meanwhile, white American soldiers serving in the same arenas treated Black soldiers abroad like second-class citizens, just as they had at home in the United States.

ROSIE THE RIVETER

During World War I, the slowdown of immigration from Europe to America created a labor vacuum that was ultimately filled by Black southerners, and during World War II, a similar labor vacuum was created by the number of men who were serving overseas. In their place, women entered the workforce in record numbers, staffing the assembly lines building tanks, machinery, and weaponry. The historical narrative concerning women in the workforce in the 1940s often lacks an intersectional perspective to account for people who were both women *and* Black. As a result, many texts on the subject portray the 1940s as a transformative point for women's equality because it "brought women out of the home and into

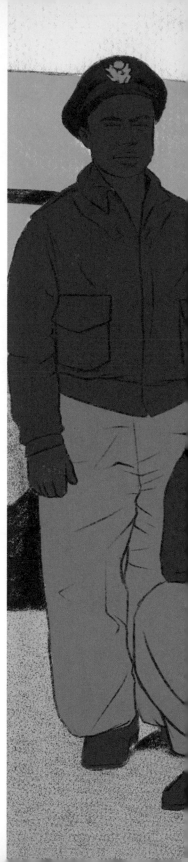

Tuskegee Airmen >>

the workforce." However, Black women had *always* been a part of the American workforce, beginning with chattel slavery and continuing into sharecropping and domestic work. Despite this reality, American society did not deem women in the workplace as cause for celebration until *after* white women began to go to work. When America entered the war in 1941, many Black women left their jobs as domestic workers and sought better-paying jobs in aircraft manufacturing, which had the highest volume of women workers during the war. In Los Angeles, my grandmother Eloise, who was seventeen, began working at the Lockheed factory in 1942 on the assembly line along with her mother, Macie, who continued her work as a beautician on the weekends. While white women were paid less than white men, Black women were paid less than Black men *and* white women, often necessitating that they work multiple jobs to make ends meet.

The influx of women working in aircraft manufacturing motivated the creation of Rosie the Riveter, a character aimed at inspiring women to join the war effort. While historical narratives claim that all women during this time period had more access to different careers in science, medicine, and journalism, the reality is that Black women were ushered to domestic, agricultural, and some of the most risky and dangerous positions available, just as they had been historically. Due to discrimination and white women's complicity in a white supremacist system, many Black women struggled to maintain manufacturing jobs as white women often refused to work alongside them. At the Baltimore Western Electric plant, for example, white women demanded that the company build segregated bathrooms for Black and white workers.

As more and more American men left home to serve abroad, more American women took on industrial jobs. While a growing number of women went to work during the war, they were simultaneously expected to continue caring for their homes and families. Wartime rationing forced women to meticulously plan meals, because grocery lists were ultimately dictated by the government. The ration book slogan "If you don't need it, DON'T BUY IT" captured the popular sentiment of American consumers. Newspapers and magazines began to shame women for raising "latchkey children," who were unsupervised for the majority of the day while their parents worked. These same newspapers simultaneously urged that victory could only be secured if women joined the workforce. For a brief period,

America considered addressing the need for child care for women workers. In 1943, the American government released funding for day-care centers across the United States through the Lanham Act (1940). Demand was extremely high, and government funding did not fully address the need. By the end of World War II, the U.S. Congress refused to renew funding for child care, and factories laid off women and Black people en masse to replace them with their preferred type of employee, white men. When veterans returned from the war, it was routine for companies to return the jobs that "rightfully belonged" to them.

White women, who had been able to serve in their own Air Corps—which was segregated by both race and gender and where they were called Women Airforce Service Pilots (WASPs)—also fell victim to this prioritization of men. The Air Corps trained over one thousand white women pilots, but the unit was dissolved after just a year, with military leaders reminding white women of their place within the patriarchy. On October 1, 1944, after the WASPs were to be disbanded, the Army Air Force headquarters issued a telegram addressed to the entire unit: "You have freed male pilots for other work, but now the war situation has changed and the time has come when your volunteered services are no longer needed . . . if you continue in service, you will be replacing . . . our young men." This attitude toward women was very common following the war, as women of all races who had been employed during the war were forced to leave the workforce. Black women returned to domestic and service work, while many white women left the workforce completely.

THE AFTERMATH OF WORLD WAR II

When the war ended in September 1945, Black Americans struggled with the continued deferment of equality. Black Americans returning from World War II came home to little recognition of their service and achievements and to numerous barriers that prevented them from rebuilding their lives. These Black American veterans had fought Nazis overseas and had sacrificed their lives under the promise that they were fighting for freedom. Returning home to civilian life made it clear that "freedom" was a long way off for the Black community. Black veterans from the prestigious Tuskegee Airmen to the enlisted men and

Of the one million
Black people who joined
the workforce during
World War II, 60 percent
were Black women.

women who had held administrative and service positions were shut out from the American dream, as if they had been the enemy and not the protector. Black soldiers who had served abroad were, for the most part, treated as equals to their European and North African counterparts overseas. Returning home to the United States where "separate but equal" made segregation constitutional presented a jarring culture shock for many Black veterans who once again were forced to grapple with being second-class citizens in the so-called land of the free.

During the war, America had portrayed itself as the antithesis of Hitler's Germany, but racism and prejudice continued to be realities of everyday life in the United States. From propaganda to policy, the United States demonstrated a clear disdain for people of color. Jewish refugees who sought sanctuary in America were routinely denied. After the Japanese military attack on Pearl Harbor, the American press began portraying Japan as a nation of subhuman creatures. And while America was condemning the egregious brutality of Hitler's concentration camps and the Holocaust, it held Japanese Americans and immigrants in internment camps. The waves of anti-Japanese propaganda allowed the U.S. military to exert morally reprehensible actions against Japanese people, including the mass murder of civilians in Hiroshima and Nagasaki, with the enthusiastic support of the American people.

The "us" versus "them" narrative of World War II excluded Americans of color, often framing them as the enemy. These attitudes ultimately shaped life after the war as hate crimes persisted. For Black World War II veteran John C. Jones and his cousin Albert Harris Jr., returning home did not come with any of the honor, valor, or respect afforded to white G.I.s of the era. In 1946 in Louisiana, the cousins were accused of trespassing in a neighbor's yard. Over the following day, the two were arrested, beaten, and released. With no civil rights protections or infrastructure to root out police corruption or vigilante hate groups, the two were attacked again, and Jones was killed. His murder highlighted the ways that life and liberty were being denied to Black people. The NAACP led an investigation, and the Justice Department also looked into the wrongful death, but no one was ever held accountable for this egregious act. Black newspapers circulated the story, as well as the stories of subsequent vigilante murders and lynchings that inspired even more Black southerners to take refuge in the North and the West.

In 1944, the U.S. Congress passed the Servicemen's Readjustment Act, also called the G.I. Bill, hoping to avoid the massive unemployment that followed World War I. The bill would provide free education, housing, and job training to returning soldiers who had served for 120 days or more of active duty. Some Black and queer veterans were barred from accessing any veteran benefits, including those from the G.I. Bill, after being issued arbitrary blue discharge papers, which dismissed them from military service. Between 1941 and 1945, approximately 22 percent of the more than 48,000 blue discharge papers issued by the U.S. Army were issued to Black soldiers, who constituted less than 7 percent of the Army. For those Black soldiers who were able to access the G.I. Bill, benefits were not evenly distributed across race, because there was no infrastructure in place to protect against discrimination. For example, as Black veterans sought jobs on assembly lines, some companies largely shut their doors to Black people, while others offered a pittance for pay. When Black G.I.s did not accept substandard jobs, their unemployment benefits promised by the G.I. Bill were terminated for failure to accept job offers.

Black people were also unable to benefit from the postwar housing boom, which was created by the economic prosperity of the era. Black veterans could secure affordable mortgages on paper, but in practice, they could not persuade banks to provide loans for homes in Black neighborhoods. Enterprising housing developers planted cookie-cutter homes across the United States as they created suburbs; however, discrimination prevented Black people from accessing this new wealth. Among these white housing developers was William Levitt, who built homes on Long Island, New York, and in the surrounding area that became known as Levittown. As was the case across the country, leases on Levitt's houses included rules that barred people of color from being able to buy or even occupy these homes. A quote from a standard Levittown lease stated, "Levittown homes must not be occupied by any person other than members of the Caucasian race." Seventy years after Levittown was created, fewer than 1 percent of its residents are Black. In fact, the deed to my grandmother's house in California, which she purchased in 1962, came with a defunct 1945 deed that prohibited the sale of the house to "Negro, Mongoloid, and Mexican persons."

These racist policies were perpetuated at the federal level: the Federal Housing Administration (FHA) advised homeowners that more than two families of color in an otherwise white neighborhood could destroy the real estate values of a community. The government also generated guiding maps, where neighborhoods outlined in red were bad and those outlined in green were good. This practice became known as redlining, and unsurprisingly, the maps also correlated to where Black and white communities had settled. While white veterans were given assistance from the government to buy homes and build long-term financial stability or wealth, Black veterans faced barriers to accessing these opportunities. Redlining resulted in 98 percent of the housing loans between 1934 and 1968 going to white families.

In the United States, homeownership was a major force in wealth accumulation, and because of these racist barriers, Black families were denied the ability to make these crucial investments while white families had numerous advantages. Today, the average Black family's income is about 60 percent that of a white family's average income, but Black wealth is just 5 to 7 percent of white wealth. According to Richard Rothstein of the Economic Policy Institute, this difference is "almost entirely attributable to federal housing policies implemented through the 20th century" from which Black Americans were excluded. Businesses, including grocery stores, department stores, and banks, were less likely to operate in redlined neighborhoods, making healthy food and jobs out of reach for most Black families. Conversely, green neighborhoods enjoyed an increase in business interests, which placed new opportunities on the doorsteps of white families. A plan that was intended to sustain the postwar economy and provide stability to returning soldiers only broadened the wealth gap between Black and white families. Many of the people who were denied access to housing, education, and jobs were returning veterans of color, and they overwhelmingly felt that this inequality was unacceptable. These attitudes of disillusionment and frustration laid the foundation of the Civil Rights movement.

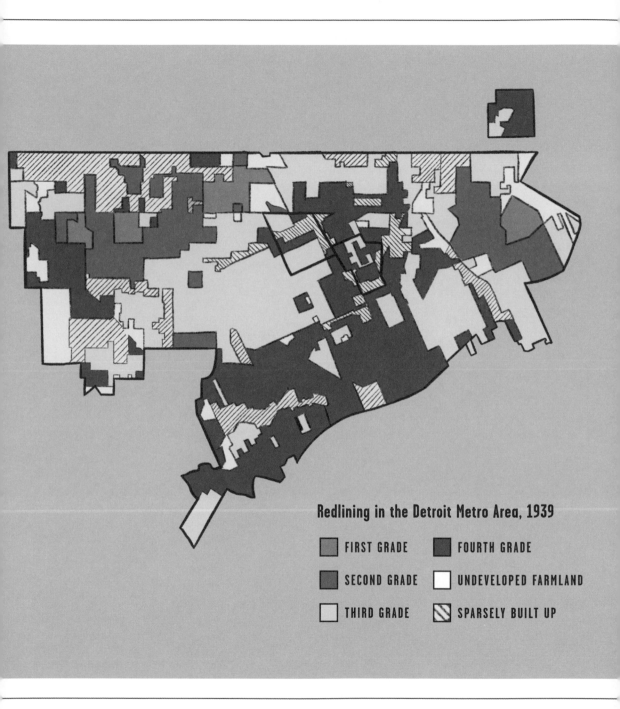

Redlining in the Detroit Metro Area, 1939

FIRST GRADE

SECOND GRADE

THIRD GRADE

FOURTH GRADE

UNDEVELOPED FARMLAND

SPARSELY BUILT UP

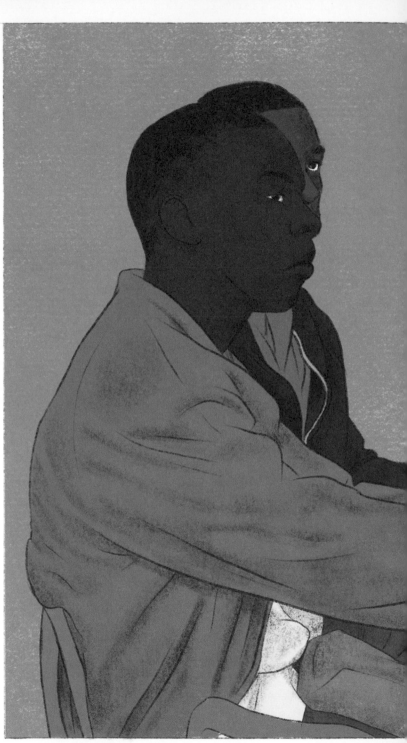

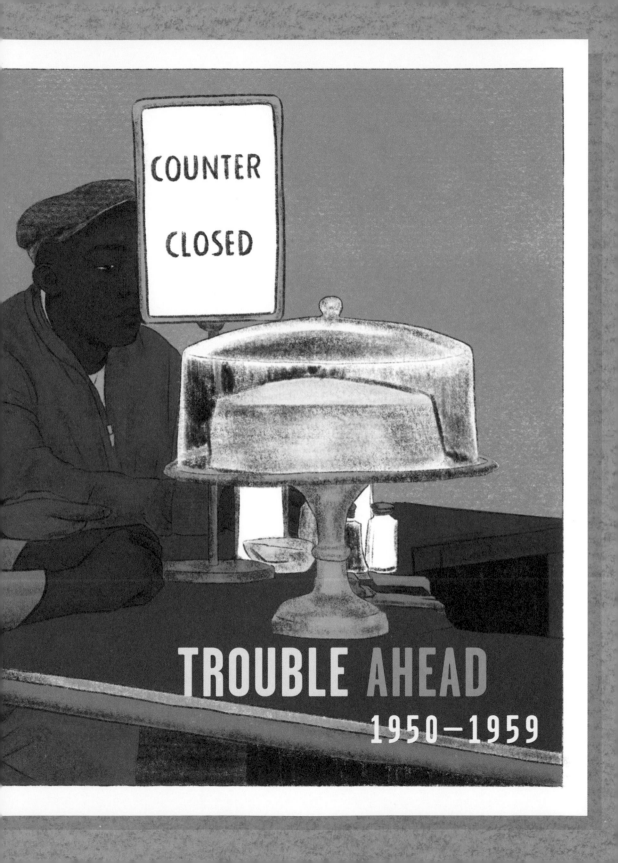

FOLLOWING WORLD WAR II, AMERICANS SETTLED IN INDUSTRIAL CITIES like Los Angeles, Baltimore, Philadelphia, New York, Detroit, and Chicago. The national unemployment rate was at a low 4.3 percent in 1950, a far cry from the 25 percent unemployment rate at the height of the Great Depression in 1933. The United States had established itself as a military and economic superpower, and millions of Americans were able to afford homes of their own. Teenagers and young adults were able to spend their free time in movie theaters, malls, bowling alleys, and malt shops that played the popular music of the day. However, this new wealth was not equally enjoyed by all Americans. The median family income in 1950 was $3,319 (or $35,009, adjusted for today's dollars), but this erased the harsh reality of life for Black Americans and other Americans of color whose median income was $1,869 (or $19,714 when adjusted for today's dollars).

Still, increased income meant that Black people were able to buy cars. Black people took to the recently constructed highways and interstates both to relocate their families and to enjoy leisurely road trips. Even in personal cars, however, the Black community could not escape the designation of second-class citizen. Without prior warning, a traveling Black family would have no way of knowing whether a given gas station, restroom, restaurant, or inn would allow them to set foot on the premises. Fortunately, a Harlem postal worker named Victor Hugo Green started publishing *The Negro Motorist Green Book* in 1936 to catalog dining and lodging establishments across America for Black motorists who were barred from segregated establishments while on the road. Green modeled his book after similar books that the Jewish community published during the 1930s. The Green Book, as it was often called, grew in popularity, reminding motorists on its front cover, "Always Carry Your Green Book with You—You May Need It." Additionally, other civil rights leaders including Medgar Evers formed a group of Black civil rights leaders in Cleveland, Mississippi, called the Regional Council of Negro Leadership, and in its first year, it distributed more than 50,000 bumper stickers with the call to action: "Don't Buy Gas Where You Can't Use the Restroom." This campaign resulted in Mississippi gas stations providing segregated restrooms for Black motorists.

The American birth rate spiked in a postwar "baby boom," spurred by the economic prosperity and optimism of the time. At the same time, the Black community became increasingly adamant that their children should have access to the American Dream, too, and modern civil rights organizing began in earnest throughout the decade. Segregation impacted every aspect of life for Black Americans—from housing and education to employment and access to public space and beyond—but its impact on Black children hadn't been formally documented. During the 1940s, two psychologists, Drs. Mamie Clark and Kenneth Clark, conducted a revolutionary series of experiments known as the doll tests to study the psychological effects of the "separate but equal" doctrine of segregation on Black children. During the tests, 253 Black children aged three to seven were presented with four otherwise identical dolls, two of which had dark skin while the other two had light skin. After preliminary questions asking the children

Thurgood Marshall

Baby boomers
were born between
World War II and
the peak of the
Civil Rights movement
(1944–1964).

Ella Baker

to identify the races of the dolls, the children were then asked to point out the "nice" dolls and "bad" dolls. Overwhelmingly, the Black children associated negative qualities with the Black dolls and showed a preference for the white dolls. Then, when asked to select the dolls most like themselves, many of the children became upset at the prospect of identifying with the "bad" Black dolls. The Clarks released their findings in 1947, but it wasn't until the early 1950s that the research gained mainstream attention, when it was used in the landmark 1954 *Brown v. Board of Education* case, which ruled segregation in public schools unconstitutional.

Black people across America were determined to access the liberties the Constitution promised to all American citizens, and the 1950s saw the full blossoming of the Civil Rights movement. The National Association for the Advancement of Colored People (NAACP), alongside individuals like Thurgood Marshall, Robert Carter, and Amos Hall, worked to challenge racist policies within the courts. On June 5, 1950, the U.S. Supreme Court issued three favorable decisions in *McLaurin v. Oklahoma State Regents*, *Sweatt v. Painter*, and *Henderson v. United States*, chipping away at the flimsy basis for the *Plessy v. Ferguson* doctrine of "separate but equal" and working to lay the foundation for the *Brown v. Board of Education* case in 1954. Progress continued when the U.S. Congress, at the urging of Black civil rights leaders, established the Civil Rights Act of 1957, which resurrected the goals set out nearly a century prior during Reconstruction.

Coretta Scott King

James Baldwin and Lorraine Hansberry

The act established a new civil rights division of the Justice Department and empowered federal prosecutors to prosecute people who attempted to stop or thwart Americans from voting. These protections enabled civil rights leaders to make new strides toward equality.

Bus boycotts, campaigns for school desegregation, and the first sit-ins of the Civil Rights movement took place during the 1950s as charismatic icons of Black history like Ella Baker, Medgar Evers, Martin Luther King Jr., Coretta Scott King, El Hajj Malik El Shabazz (also known as Malcolm X), Lorraine Hansberry, and James Baldwin emerged on the national stage, becoming household names as freedom fighters, activists, artists, and religious leaders.

THE CIVIL RIGHTS MOVEMENT

Traditionally, 1954 is cited as the year that marks the start of the Civil Rights movement, but the seeds of this movement had been planted decades prior. When the *Plessy v. Ferguson* case established the "separate but equal" doctrine in 1896, segregation governed the lives of Black Americans and people of color in the United States. Everything from public transportation to health care, education, and housing was segregated and far from equal. Sixty years after the *Plessy v. Ferguson* case, it still had lasting implications. During the 1950s, segregation was mandated in seventeen southern states, while it was permitted or limited in four other states. The remaining states had outlawed segregation or did not have formal segregation polices in place at all. In 1952, the average spending on white students was 50 percent more than spending on students of color in southern states. It was very clear to Black parents that their children were not being provided the equal opportunity they needed to succeed.

By 1950, the NAACP had four hundred thousand members, and it began working on a strategy to systematically dismantle the legal basis for racial segregation. With Thurgood Marshall at the helm, the organization's local chapters worked to enlist parents who would be willing to enroll their children in all-white schools. The parents and civil rights leaders knew that these attempts would be stopped, but they also knew that these actions would set up the basis for legal action. In 1951, Topeka, Kansas, NAACP leaders Charles Scott and Lucinda Todd recruited Oliver Brown to enroll his daughter Linda Brown in an all-white school in Topeka. The segregated white school was significantly closer to the Brown family home than the Black school that the school district forced her to attend. Unsurprisingly, when Brown attempted to enroll his daughter in the white school, he was denied. Expecting such a turn of events, the local NAACP brought a class action lawsuit against the school district; the lawsuit, listing Oliver Brown as the primary plaintiff, included twenty Black students and thirteen parents who had similarly tried to enroll in the white school. The civil rights lawyers argued that the Topeka Board of Education was denying students their constitutional right to equal protection as guaranteed by the Fourteenth Amendment. During the initial *Brown v. Board of Education* case, the district court in the state of Kansas declared that the schools in question were of equal condition and qualification, despite being segregated on the basis of race. Undeterred, the NAACP challenged this ruling at the highest court in the land, the U.S. Supreme Court. Thurgood Marshall argued the case, and on May 17, 1954, the all-white panel of Supreme Court judges unanimously decided to overturn the *Plessy v. Ferguson* (1896) "separate but equal" doctrine. The fight was far from over, because the ruling in *Brown v. Board of Education* (1954) simply ordered state attorneys general to integrate American schools "with all deliberate speed" but did not provide any means of enforcement or accountability.

Three years after this decision, nine students from Little Rock, Arkansas, volunteered with a local chapter of the NAACP to be the first students to integrate the all-white Little Rock Central High School. The nine students, called the Little Rock Nine, included Ernest Green, Elizabeth Eckford, Jefferson Thomas, Terrence Roberts, Carlotta Walls LaNier, Minnijean Brown, Gloria Ray Karlmark, Thelma Mothershed, and Melba Pattillo Beals. While *Brown v. Board of Education* had indeed declared segregation to be unconstitutional and a violation of the equal protection clause in the Fourteenth Amendment, attempts to act on this new ruling sparked outrage from white communities. Upon the first attempt by the Little Rock Nine to enter Central High School, white parents and community members erupted into a raging mob, spitting on, hitting, and yelling at the young Black teenagers. For three weeks, the Arkansas National Guard prevented the Little Rock Nine from attending school on the orders of Arkansas governor Orval Faubus. By the end of September 1957, the nine were escorted into Central High School under the protection of the 101st Airborne Division of the U.S. Army, even while their white peers subjected them to a year of physical and verbal abuse and harassment. During the following 1958–1959 school year, Governor Faubus closed Central High School to put integration attempts there to an end. Out of the nine brave students, three would graduate from Central high School with others seeking to continue their education elsewhere. The Little Rock Nine demonstrated the power of youth action and courage to go against the mainstream even at immense personal sacrifice.

One year before the landmark decision made in *Brown v. Board of Education* (1954), Black Americans in the city of Baton Rouge, Louisiana, launched the first bus boycott of the Civil Rights movement. In 1950, the Baton Rouge City Council had voted to ban Black-owned bus companies in the city. At the time, there was little legal recourse for everyday Black people, who relied on those Black-owned bus companies to get them to and from work and school every day. Black people in Baton Rouge comprised 80 percent of the ridership of those buses; under the new system, Black people would have to try their luck riding in the back of segregated buses that prioritized seating for white passengers. Even if a bus's section for white passengers was empty, Black people could not occupy those seats. Furthermore, they were forced to vacate the bus entirely and walk the rest of the way to their destination if additional white passengers needed to overflow into the Black section. For three years, Black children, women, and men suffered these unjust conditions until 1953, when Black Baton Rougeans organized the first boycott of a southern city's segregated bus system. The boycott ultimately ended when city leaders reached a compromise with the bus companies, wherein the companies decreased the number of white-only seats to accommodate the higher number of Black passengers. While the Baton Rouge bus boycott did not end in a complete victory against segregation on buses, it did demonstrate that there was trouble ahead for racist institutions.

Even after *Brown v. Board of Education*, segregation in many public spaces continued. In 1955, fifteen-year-old Claudette Colvin, pregnant at the time, was arrested for refusing to give up her seat on a segregated Montgomery, Alabama, bus to a white woman. Claudette Colvin was a member of the NAACP Youth Council and felt empowered by the growing movement for civil rights. Colvin was not working as a protester or planning to take an arrest for strategic purposes. Nonetheless, Colvin's refusal to comply with the racist laws in Montgomery inspired additional acts of resistance, including that of NAACP regional secretary Rosa Parks, who was arrested for civil disobedience months later in order to craft a sympathetic public narrative. One month after Colvin's defiant act in the same city, thirty-six-year-old Aurelia Browder was also arrested for refusing to give up her seat to a white passenger. In February 1956, four women, including Colvin and Browder, alongside seventy-year-old Susie McDonald and eighteen-year-old Mary Louise Smith—who had all been arrested for refusing to submit to a racist system—joined a federal civil case called *Browder v. Gayle* to challenge bus segregation in Alabama. While Rosa Parks is remembered for being the catalyst for the desegregation of buses in Alabama, the Montgomery Bus Boycott, which began after Rosa Parks's 1955 arrest, could not have happened without the sacrifices of Colvin, Browder, McDonald, and Smith and the learnings from the earlier Baton Rouge bus boycotts. In 1956, the U.S. Supreme Court upheld the lower court's decision in *Browder v. Gayle* that ordered Alabama to desegregate buses, thus inspiring similar efforts in other states.

While some progress was beginning to take hold, violence against Black people was still rampant. In August 1955, a teenager named Emmett Till traveled from his home in Chicago to visit relatives in Mississippi. Mamie Till, Emmett's mother, had been born in Mississippi and moved to Chicago for improved access

Claudette Colvin

Rosa Parks

to jobs. On August 28, Carolyn Bryant Donham completely fabricated a story that fourteen-year-old Till had harassed her by whistling as she walked past. Days later, three white men, including Donham's husband, abducted Till from his uncle's home. By nightfall, fourteen-year-old Till had been beaten, disfigured, and murdered before being dumped into the Tallahatchie river. Till's body was discovered three days later; his face was so badly disfigured that he could be identified only by the ring on his finger. Till's mother requested that his body be sent back to Chicago, where she insisted on holding an open casket funeral so the world could see what had been done to her child. *Jet* magazine, a Black publication, published a photo of Till's badly disfigured body, and the story was heard around the world. Till's murderers never faced justice, because an all-white jury issued a

Emmett Till and Mamie Till

"not guilty" verdict after deliberating for only one hour. In 2017, Timothy B. Tyson's book *The Blood of Emmett Till* revealed that Donham had admitted that the story she had repeated to investigators and the media for sixty years had been a complete lie. Her lie resulted in the brutal murder of a fourteen-year-old boy and demonstrated the role that white women played in maintaining a racist society. Following the murder, many Black families in Mississippi, who were able to do so, decided to move north in the hopes that their children would not succumb to Emmett Till's fate.

CIVIL RIGHTS LEADERS

Following the landmark victories of the early 1950s, expert organizers who had worked both in communities and in well-established civil rights organizations like the NAACP came together to birth new coalitions to work toward freedom. Veteran organizers like Bayard Rustin, Ella Baker, and A. Philip Randolph worked with emerging leaders like Dr. Martin Luther King Jr., Coretta Scott King, and Medgar Evers to provide guidance and mentorship as they worked across the South. In 1957, following the successes during the Montgomery bus boycotts, the *Brown v. Board of Education* decision, and the Little Rock Nine school integration, Bayard Rustin, Ella Baker, and Martin Luther King Jr. convened at the Ebenezer Church in Atlanta to establish the Southern Christian Leadership Conference (SCLC) to continue efforts in civil rights organizing.

Bayard Rustin was an openly gay Black civil rights leader who had worked alongside labor organizer A. Philip Randolph to organize the unrealized 1941 March on Washington, whose goal was to push for an end to discrimination in the workplace. The march was deemed unnecessary when FDR signed Executive Order 8802 barring racial discrimination in the U.S. defense industry. A year later, Rustin supported the formation of the Congress of Racial Equality (CORE), which was founded by James L. Farmer Jr. and George Houser in Chicago in March 1942. While Rustin is often cited as a civil rights leader, his identity as a gay man is often erased, although in life he maintained that "it was an absolute necessity for me to declare homosexuality because if I didn't I was a part of the prejudice." Rustin would be instrumental in the organization of the 1963 March on Washington and of the Freedom Rides, which were based on initial efforts by CORE in the 1947 Journey of Reconciliation.

Ella Baker became the connective tissue of the Civil Rights movement because she had served as the NAACP director of branches during the 1940s. Baker had civil rights organizer contacts in nearly every major city across the country, and she used those contacts to form lasting coalitions. Baker believed that "the young people were the hope of any movement," and she was adamant that the movement toward freedom adopt a structure of decentralized leadership. In 1960, while serving as executive secretary for the SCLC, Baker founded the first organized

Martin Luther King Jr. speaking with Rosa Parks and other members of the SCLC.

Medgar Evers

conference of the Student Nonviolent Coordinating Committee (SNCC) at Shaw University in Raleigh, North Carolina. Baker prioritized the emerging youth voices with a call to action, stating, "Adult Freedom Fighters will be present for counsel and guidance, but the meeting will be youth centered."

The Civil Rights movement did not exclusively take place in the South. In Detroit, Chicago, Los Angeles, and Harlem, New York, the Nation of Islam began attracting Black people from all walks of life, with teachings based on Pan-Africanism, self-reliance, sobriety, healthy eating, and family values. The Nation of Islam promoted the economic and political independence of Black people, teaching them how to buy land and open businesses, such as grocery stores and barbershops, and training the organization's youth in community protection tactics. Like the teachings of Marcus Garvey, the Nation of Islam advocates for the creation of a separate state in America that, unlike the U.S. government, focuses on the needs of the Black community. Members were encouraged to discard the remnants of chattel slavery, such as last names that had come from slave owners. This process of self-naming had its roots in Reconstruction, when formerly enslaved people chose new last names or took the name Freeman. Under the guidance of spiritual leader Elijah Muhammad, the group attracted a twenty-seven-year-old man who would become known to the world as Malcolm X (and later as El Hajj Malik El Shabazz once he cut ties with the Nation of Islam and joined Sunni Islam). After joining the Nation of Islam in 1952, Shabazz rose to prominence and was eventually appointed as leader of the Nation of Islam temples in Boston and Harlem. As a speaker and cultural force, Shabazz used mass media like newspapers, radio, and television to spread messages of self-reliance and Black empowerment. From 1952 to 1963, membership in the Nation of Islam grew from five hundred to thirty thousand, and many historians cite Shabazz's influence for this dramatic growth.

As the Civil Rights movement gained momentum, J. Edgar Hoover launched the Federal Bureau of Investigation (FBI)'s Counterintelligence Program, better known as COINTELPRO, in 1956. The program's goal was to gather intelligence on and destabilize Black civil rights organizations often through illegal means. Civil rights organizations and their leaders were already responsible for immense changes in society. With virtually no support from the U.S. government, the NAACP, with the support of Black publications and similar organizations, had dismantled segregation in schools, industries, public accommodations, and on public transportation. Hoover and many other leaders within the U.S. government wanted to retain the power that had been held by white people for centuries, and they felt threatened by these advancements. Just as Marcus Garvey had earlier become the target of the FBI, so, too, did Martin Luther King Jr., El Hajj Malik El Shabazz, and countless other civil rights leaders.

POPULAR CULTURE

With free time in abundance and record players at the ready, music played a
major role in shaping the culture of the 1950s. Black American culture helped
shape the new musical genres of rock 'n' roll and doo-wop that became massively
popular even as Black people and other communities of color still struggled for
basic civil rights.

Doo-wop, a term that did not emerge to describe the genre until its popularity
had started to decline in the 1960s, was characterized by instrumental-backed
vocals about romance and love. Black doo-wop quartets emerged as some of
the first boy bands, and, unsurprisingly, many emerged in places where Black

Sister Rosetta Tharpe

communities were concentrated in the 1950s. In Los Angeles, the Platters rose to prominence, and the Penguins followed suit with their chart-topping song "Earth Angel," and in Chicago, the Flamingos captured the hearts of countless fans with "I'll Be Home." Rock 'n' roll also gained popularity during this time—it did not begin with Elvis Presley as many believe. The genre has roots in Black American gospel, blues, and soul. While Elvis may have popularized rock 'n' roll music for white audiences, the genre was shaped by Georgia-born musicians like Sister Rosetta Tharpe and Little Richard, as well as St. Louis legend Chuck Berry. The public reaction to Black singers during the 1950s directly mirrored social attitudes toward Black people during the era. Just as jazz and blues had in Harlem during the 1920s and 1930s, rock 'n' roll music attracted mixed audiences; this angered racist organizations like the White Citizens' Council, which opposed bringing different races together. Conservative Black communities also warned against listening to rock 'n' roll, not because of its power to bring people together across race, but because it commercialized many of the gospel sounds that people of faith in the community held sacred. As with rap music today, the more adults warned of rock 'n' roll's supposed dangers, the more intensely teenagers gravitated to the music. Rock 'n' roll represented the limitless nature of creative self-expression for American teenagers during a time when social conformity was a highly valued norm. Not surprisingly, rock 'n' roll soon became synonymous with teenage rebellion.

Black solo artists like Ray Charles, James Brown, and Little Richard filled the airwaves and joined ranks with Black actors like Harry Belafonte, Lena Horne, and Dorothy Dandridge, who were gracing stages and screens. Television became a cultural fixture during the 1950s, and it also became a battleground for integration and acceptance. In 1956, Nat King Cole became the first Black American performer to host a variety TV series called *The Nat King Cole Show*. Cole was born in Montgomery, Alabama, and during his teenage years, he and his family moved to Chicago with countless other families during the Great Migration Although the show was only fifteen minutes long in its first iteration, Cole's presence on screen was a triumph for many in the Black community. In 1953, Harry Belafonte debuted alongside Dorothy Dandridge in the film *Bright Road*, and the two went on to play opposite each other in additional films. Even though the films were in black and white, colorism dictated the opportunities to which Black actors had access. Hattie McDaniel, for example, a dark-skinned Black woman, was relegated to roles portraying enslaved people, and even though she won an academy award in 1939 for her portrayal of Mammy in *Gone with the Wind*, it was clear that Hollywood made more room for Black actors with fairer skin. While Harry Belafonte enjoyed his status as a sex symbol, his darker-skinned contemporary, Sidney Poitier, was not imbued with this same status of desirability. Lena Horne later discussed the twisted acceptance she experienced with white audiences because of colorism. Black publications like *Ebony*, which was founded in 1945, defied this pattern of colorism and granted glossy full-color covers throughout the decade to Black people of all shades.

Literary figures built upon the foundations created by the 1920s Harlem Renaissance movement and also contributed to the cultural landscape of the 1950s. James Baldwin was born in 1924 at the height of the Harlem Renaissance in New York City. In 1953, as Black Americans in the South worked to desegregate public transportation, James Baldwin published a compelling memoir titled *Go Tell It On The Mountain*, which provided a much-needed perspective into the intricacies of Black identity and humanity. Lorraine Hansberry, who was born in 1930 in Chicago, drew upon her experiences with racism in childhood to write the play *The Crystal Stair*. Later, the play was renamed *A Raisin in the Sun* to pay homage to Harlem Renaissance poet Langston Hughes. The title of the play was taken from the poem "Harlem" by Langston Hughes: "What happens to a dream deferred? Does it dry up like a raisin in the sun?" In 1959, *A Raisin in the Sun* became the first play produced on Broadway by a Black woman and garnered critical acclaim. Works by Baldwin and Hansberry allowed white audiences to step into the shoes of everyday Black Americans, and for the Black community, their work symbolized milestones in the accurate and mainstream portrayal of the Black American experience.

Although Black people were hugely influential in shaping the popular culture of the 1950s, they were often unable to financially benefit from their work. Many artists who had emerged during the Harlem Renaissance were not able to establish long-term financial security, and the recording industry was predominantly white and unwilling to take chances on Black recording artists. In Detroit,

Little Richard >>

Chuck Berry

THE MAN WHO CRACKED
THE BRINK'S CASE

GI RISKS DEATH
65 TIMES FOR SCIENCE

A JOHNSON PUBLICATION

Mr. and Mrs. Sidney Poitier

HOLLYWOOD'S
FIRST NEGRO
MOVIE STAR

Cover of *Ebony*, May 1959

entrepreneur and Korean War veteran Berry Gordy had a vision to rectify this injustice, and his work would come to shape the soulful sounds associated with the 1960s and 1970s. In the heart of the Motor City in 1959, Gordy established Tamla Records, later known as Motown Records. As a songwriter during the 1950s, Gordy received a paltry royalty check of $3.19 and swiftly became convinced that Black artists needed to be able to benefit financially from the growing interest in Black music. Gordy crowdfunded $800 with his family to establish his company decades before the era of online crowdfunding. Using this initial investment, Gordy created a new kind of assembly line in Detroit, one that made hit songs instead of cars. Entertainment continued to be a way for Black Americans to lift themselves to new heights.

THE TIME IS
IN THE STREET,
YOU KNOW

1960–1969

BLACK CHILDREN AND TEENAGERS BORN DURING THE 1940S AND 1950S were raised on the accomplishments of the early Civil Rights movement and had access to these historic moments through film, television, and radio. Witnessing these landmark changes in American society empowered people who were young, gifted, and Black to contribute to the Civil Rights movement and make it their own. Across the United States, decades-old organizations like the National Association for the Advancement of Colored People (NAACP), founded in 1909, and the Congress of Racial Equality (CORE), founded in 1942, joined forces with new youth-led groups to reach new heights of political organizing during the 1960s.

During James Meredith's March Against Fear on June 16, 1966, Trinidadian-American activist Kwame Ture, president of the Student Nonviolent Coordinating Committee (SNCC), gave a powerful speech in which he called for "Black Power." While the earliest use of the phrase was in Richard Wright's 1954 book *Black Power*, Ture's ideology focused on the establishment of cultural, political, and social institutions that uplift and promote the needs and interests of the Black community. As a political ideology and as a cultural force, Black Power came to represent a shifting approach toward civil rights organizing. While the early Civil Rights movement focused on dismantling oppressive institutions like segregation, the Black Power movement focused on uplifting and healing the Black community.

Black Power made its way into the world of popular culture, beauty, and fashion in the form of the Black is Beautiful movement. While artists like Langston Hughes had asserted that Blackness was beautiful decades prior in the 1920s, "Black is Beautiful" was still a revolutionary statement within the context of white supremacy. For centuries, the American beauty standard had erased Black people's bodies, features, skin color, and hair. Slender and pointed noses, thin lips, pale skin, and straight hair were routinely favored in place of broad and rounded noses, thick lips, ebony skin, and tightly coiled locks. These Eurocentric expectations of beauty continue today and even influence self-expression within communities of color. As the Black is Beautiful movement liberated chemically processed hair and shaved-down locks, it gave rise to afros and other natural hairstyles. More importantly, it replaced the internalized notions of inferiority

The Supremes

(which had been perpetuated by segregation and discrimination) and replaced it with pride. In 1968, James Brown released "Say It Loud—I'm Black and I'm Proud," and the song quickly gained popularity within the growing Black Power and Black is Beautiful movements. In 1966, Ron Karenga created Kwanzaa as a Pan-African holiday centering Black people and the seven key values he believed were central to African heritage. Pan-Africanism, the belief that members of the African diaspora have common interests and should be unified, became a fixture within Black American consciousness.

Out of Detroit, new musicians from the large Black community entered into Motown Record's famed "assembly line" of music created by Berry Gordy. The majority of Motown's artists had roots in the American South because of the Great Migration. The discriminatory practice known as redlining and the lack of affordable housing available to Black people meant that many of Motown's artists lived in the same public housing accommodations as they had before achieving fame and fortune. Iconic figures like Diana Ross, Florence Ballard, and Mary Wilson of Motown's world-renowned The Supremes each ended up in Detroit after their families moved north in pursuit of the well-paying jobs available to Black people in the Motor City.

The 1960s saw society questioning nearly every social convention, and free creative expression continued to be an avenue for political expression. Communities of color worked together during this era to advocate for civil rights and the rights of workers serving in agricultural positions as well. Although the economy following World War II had brought many southern farmworkers to industrial jobs in the 1950s and 1960s, many newcomers from Mexico, the Philippines, and the South could only find employment cultivating farmland on the West Coast. In 1962, the United Farm Workers of America (UFWA), founded by Dolores Huerta, Cesar Chavez, and Larry Itliong, united farmworkers from the Black, Chicano, Filipino, and Mexican communities. Through direct action and persistent union organizing, the UFWA increased the wages of farmworkers and demonstrated the power of building collective action across communities.

Amid the progress, Black people grappled with continued disillusionment toward institutions and systems that denied basic freedoms and opportunities to their communities. These frustrations reached a critical point when Black civil rights leaders Medgar Evers, El Hajj Malik El Shabazz (also known as Malcolm X), Dr. Martin Luther King Jr., and Fred Hampton had all been assassinated by the end of the decade. Contrary to popular belief, the Civil Rights movement did not die with these great leaders, but rather it continued and transformed with the needs of the people. Leaders like Kwame Ture and emerging groups such as the Black Panther Party took up the reins to continue the fight for freedom.

Dr. Martin Luther King Jr. and El Hajj Malik El Shabazz

POWER TO THE PEOPLE

From 1960 to 1966, Black migration accounted for approximately 34 percent of urban growth. Although Black people were leaving the South, twelve million Black people still called the South home by the 1970s. The Black community recognized that migrating away from the South was not a permanent solution to American racism and segregation, so many continued the fight in the courts and on the streets. On February 1, 1960, four Black students bravely took seats at a segregated lunch counter in Greensboro, North Carolina. In asking to be served a meal, they were not fighting for the right to eat sandwiches next to white people, they were fighting to be seen, treated, and served as equals. Although the "separate but equal" doctrine had been struck down by the U.S. Supreme Court in 1954, Jim Crow laws still kept a vice grip on the lives of Black people across the South throughout the 1950s and into the 1960s. Black people could not be served at the same lunch counters as white people, they could not access mixed spaces but had to enter through different entrances, and public buses were still segregated in many states, even though its legality had been challenged since 1946. With the Great Migration in full swing, activists were adamant that hungry and traveling families should be able to utilize interstate transportation and public accommodations without fear of reproach.

In the spring of 1961, CORE and the SNCC recruited a group of Black and white bus riders to test the U.S. Supreme Court's decision in *Boynton v. Virginia* (1960), which found the segregation of interstate buses and bus stations to be unconstitutional. This demonstration, which relied heavily on the use of nonviolent civil disobedience, was modeled on the 1947 Journey of Reconciliation, which had been organized by CORE. Under the leadership of SNCC's Diane Nash and CORE's James Farmer, a group of Black and white participants set out from Washington, D.C.'s Greyhound and Trailways bus stations on May 4, 1961, to draw attention to the ways that civil rights laws were not being enforced.

In the initial plan, Freedom Riders were to travel across the South on the regular interstate bus route and meet in New Orleans for a celebratory rally. While the organizers had court declarations on their side, local Jim Crow laws and public opinion were strongly against them. The first Freedom Riders included seven

John Lewis

Black riders and six white riders and consisted of student activists and elders like Catherine Burks, Glenda Gaither, John Lewis, Kwame Ture, and Bayard Rustin. The Freedom Rides—wherein activists would peacefully ride from station to station using facilities along the way—lasted from May 4, 1961, until December 10, 1961. Like the Little Rock Nine before them, the Freedom Riders were met by mobs of angry white people ready to commit violence in order to maintain the racist status quo. On May 14, 1961, in Anniston, Alabama, two hundred white people surrounded a Greyhound bus, forcing the driver to continue driving instead of making a routine stop at the bus station. Members of the horde followed the bus, and when its tires exploded from overheating, a bomb was thrown into the vehicle. Upon escaping, the Freedom Riders were beaten with metal pipes. Images of beaten Freedom Riders set against the backdrop of the burning Greyhound bus captured international attention, but the immense risk prompted many participants to abandon the Freedom Rides. Diane Nash, a twenty-three-year-old activist from Chicago and a member of SNCC, led the efforts to continue the rides with a group of students from Fisk University. John Lewis, who went on to become a U.S. congressman, would later note that President Barack Obama, America's first Black president, was born on August 4, 1961, in the midst of the Freedom Rides movement.

Following the Freedom Rides, the new Kennedy administration urged a "cooling down" period for civil rights organizers. The international press heavily covered the continued failures by the American government to adequately

Dr. Martin Luther King Jr.

support the human rights of African Americans and other Americans of color, much to the dissatisfaction of U.S. leaders. The United States, which was in the midst of the Cold War, could not portray itself as the land of progress and freedom so long as its most vulnerable citizens were left unprotected from hate and violence. With international pressure rising, veteran civil rights organizers Bayard Rustin and A. Philip Randolph aimed to move the Kennedy administration to action by utilizing a strategy they had developed back in 1942: a massive demonstration for civil rights in the nation's capital. As logistics were managed by youth volunteers, Rustin and Randolph enlisted major Black celebrities and leadership from five major civil rights organizations to provide speeches for the 1963 March on Washington.

On the day of the demonstration, Marian Anderson opened the day's events by singing the national anthem, followed by opening remarks from A. Philip Randolph. Likely because of homophobia, openly gay civil rights leader Bayard Rustin was excluded from the program despite being a key architect of the march. Myrlie Evers, Medgar Evers's widow, honored Black women civil rights organizers, and John Lewis of the SNCC gave a powerful speech, followed by leaders of CORE, the National Urban League, and the NAACP. When Dr. Martin Luther King Jr. took the stage, he provided brief written remarks before giving a powerful improvised speech, wherein he described his dream for the future of America. The day ended with a brief meeting with President John F. Kennedy. At the time, the March on Washington was the largest civil rights demonstration in human history, with approximately 250,000 participants. To both the American government and the American public, the movement for civil rights was a unified effort. However the Civil Rights movement was a collection of different people with different strategies working toward a common goal. Despite these landmark accomplishments, injustice and violence continued to be a reality for Black people in the United States.

In 1964, one year after the powerful March on Washington, Fannie Lou Hamer, a voting rights organizer, began to implement her plan to increase voter registration in her home state of Mississippi. In 1961, just 7 percent of Black Mississippians were registered to vote. This low voter registration percentage was sustained by voter disenfranchisement and by threats of violence from

Fannie Lou Hamer

hate groups like the Ku Klux Klan (KKK). In 1963, the KKK was responsible for the murder of four young Black girls at the 16th Street Baptist Church in Birmingham, Alabama, where a strategically placed bomb incited fear and terror in the hearts of parishioners.

Freedom could not be attained without the ability of Black people to partici-pate in the governance of the United States. As the Black community suffered and survived countless other acts of brutality in the South, Fannie Lou Hamer worked to organize the 1964 Freedom Summer in Mississippi. During the sum-mer of that year, the newly established Council of Federated Organizations (COFO)—which consisted of the Mississippi branches of SNCC, CORE, NAACP, and the Southern Christian Leadership Conference (SCLC)—recruited volunteers from across the country to canvas and register Black Mississippians even while facing threats of violence. Over the ten-week program, more than one thousand volunteers were arrested; eighty Freedom Summer workers were beaten; and more than sixty churches, Black-owned businesses, and homes were firebombed. Seven innocent people lost their lives, including three Black Mississippians who were killed by hate groups just for supporting the Civil Rights movement. During the Freedom Summer, which lasted from June through August of 1964, President Lyndon B. Johnson passed the Civil Rights Act of 1964, which opened up new possibilities for civil rights organizing in the coming years.

The Civil Rights movement was everywhere that Black communities called home. In Oakland, California, which had become an industrial center drawing in Black people from the South, the increasing cost of housing threatened to push out disadvantaged citizens. Oakland had experienced a boom in its Black community from more than eight thousand in 1940 to approximately eighty-three thousand in 1960, as more southerners moved to cities in the North and West to take jobs in shipyards and factories. Even with the passage of the 1964 Civil Rights Act, Black people across America were still systematically thwarted from accessing pathways toward success and stability.

In addition to widespread discrimination that threatened jobs, housing, and health care, Black people became the frequent targets of police violence. In October 1966, Bobby Seale and Huey P. Newton founded the Black Panther Party for Self-Defense in Oakland. Later shortened to the Black Panther Party, the organization was a community-based solution to police and vigilante violence against the Black community. The two founders had themselves arrived in Oakland as children because of the Great Migration, when their families had sought to escape the economic hardships of the South. Bobby Seale was born in Texas in 1936, and Huey P. Newton was born in Louisiana in 1942. At the dawn of the organization, Black Panther members would patrol and protect Black communities from racist violence and police violence with legally obtained and registered firearms, similar to the way that local police patrolled and protected white communities. In contemporary reporting about the Black Panther Party, members were described as militants, which was the term used to describe the opposing forces during the Vietnam War. Despite media and governmental bias

Two young people at the Black Panther Party free breakfast program

against the Black Panthers, the extensive infrastructure they created to address neglect in the Black community is still being used today—including free breakfast programs for children.

As part of the original guiding framework of the Black Panther Party, Huey P. Newton and Bobby Seale created the Black Panther Party Ten Point Program in October 1966. Many reference materials inaccurately cite the Ten Point Program or add extra text that did not appear in the original. The following text is the portion of the program titled "What We Want."

THE BLACK PANTHER PARTY
PLATFORM AND PROGRAM
WHAT WE WANT

1. We want freedom. We want power to determine the destiny of our Black Community.

2. We want full employment for our people.

3. We want an end to the robbery by the white man of our Black Community.

4. We want decent housing, fit for the shelter of human beings.

5. We want education for our people that exposes the true nature of this decadent American society. We want education that teaches us our true history and our role in the present day society.

6. We want all Black men to be exempt from military service.

7. We want an immediate end to POLICE BRUTALITY and MURDER of Black people.

8. We want freedom for all Black men held in federal, state, county and city prisons and jails.

9. We want all Black people when brought to trial to be tried in court by a jury of their peer group or people from their Black Communities, as defined by the Constitution of the United States.

10. We want land, bread, housing, education, clothing, justice and peace.

THE WAR IN VIETNAM

For more than fifty years, the American government and the U.S. military had demonstrated a total refusal to treat Black soldiers as equals despite their service in World War I, World War II, and the Korean War. The popular sentiment of Black people and Black civil rights organizations toward American involvement in the Vietnam War was one of rejection. This sentiment differed immensely from that of previous wars, which Black Americans had largely supported. However, the Vietnam War ultimately saw the highest proportion of Black military service of any war in American history—and this was not due to voluntary participation.

The draft, or the Selective Service Act, conscripted American men aged nineteen to twenty-six to military service, but there were provisions that could exempt an individual from service. Many of the exemptions boiled down to access; for example, young men from wealthy families could more easily enter college or serve in the U.S. Army Reserve to receive deferments from the draft. The children of white World War II veterans were wealthier than their Black counterparts because of the ways that white G.I.s had been able to access the benefits of the G.I. Bill. The disproportionate drafting of Black Americans felt more like an overt act of retaliation against the Black community's affinity for Black Power and conscientious objection, or the refusal to participate in the war on the basis of religious beliefs, than to their sentiments against serving in the war. In 1967 alone, 64 percent of all eligible African Americans were drafted compared to only 31 percent of eligible whites.

Heavyweight boxing champion Muhammad Ali was vocal about his objections to Black American service in Vietnam. American officials and the media widely condemned Ali because, when asked why he refused to be inducted, he asserted that there should be more solidarity with the Vietnamese who were ultimately victims of a colonial force. He further stated that his conscience would not allow him to shoot people in another country for America, which had done so much harm to his own community; Vietnam was a white man's war. In 1967, Ali was arrested for failing to serve and was stripped of his heavyweight title.

In 1967, Dr. Martin Luther King Jr. made an appeal to end the American investment in waging war abroad in Vietnam and in the destabilization of governments

El Hajj Malik El Shabazz, Betty Shabazz, and their children with Muhammad Ali

in South America. He delivered a speech titled "Beyond Vietnam: A Time to Break Silence" on April 4, 1967, at Riverside Church in New York City. This speech, combined with the SNCC's increased advocacy against the draft, distinguished the war in Vietnam as one of the most opposed wars by the Black community. Dr. King said:

> A true revolution of values will soon look uneasily on the glaring contrast of poverty and wealth. With righteous indignation, it will look across the seas and see individual capitalists of the West investing huge

sums of money in Asia, Africa, and South America, only to take the prof-
its out with no concern for the social betterment of the countries, and
say, "This is not just." It will look at our alliance with the landed gentry
of South America and say, "This is not just." The Western arrogance of
feeling that it has everything to teach others and nothing to learn from
them is not just.

A true revolution of values will lay hand on the world order and say
of war, "This way of settling differences is not just." This business
of burning human beings with napalm, of filling our nation's homes
with orphans and widows, of injecting poisonous drugs of hate into
the veins of peoples normally humane, of sending men home from dark
and bloody battlefields physically handicapped and psychologically
deranged, cannot be reconciled with wisdom, justice, and love. A nation
that continues year after year to spend more money on military defense
than on programs of social uplift is approaching spiritual death.

Exactly one year after delivering this speech, an assassin murdered Dr. King
in Memphis, Tennessee.

During the war in Vietnam, Black and white soldiers served together in
integrated units, a change that civil rights organizations had successfully fought
for in previous decades. Despite the fact that soldiers were serving side by side in
integrated units, racism persisted at war and at home. It was common for white
American soldiers to use anti-Black slurs to describe the opposing forces. Any
semblance of harmony between soldiers of color and their white counterparts
often evaporated upon returning home. Black veterans recall situations where
white soldiers who had previously been their friends on the battlefield no longer
acknowledged them once they returned to America.

Collapsing friendships were not all that awaited Black veterans when they
returned home from Vietnam. The failures of the G.I. Bill had not been recti-
fied, and so the distribution of wealth among veterans continued to fall along
racial lines. For example, Vietnam War veteran and historian Gregory Hawkins
was alerted that he would be provided only 30 percent of the disability benefits
afforded to white soldiers after he was wounded in combat. Only after he wrote

to his congressman was he able to receive 40 percent of the total benefits given to white G.I.s. Like the World War II veterans before him, Hawkins was also unable to circumvent the racism of the housing system, having to prove more income than white soldiers to buy the same home. Most of the Black veterans returning from the Vietnam War were unable to move forward to benefit from the American dream.

A DREAM DEFERRED

Beginning with the assassination of Medgar Evers in 1963, it seemed that every two years there was yet another blow to the leadership of the Civil Rights movement. Many young people, like my father, grew up with comic books like *Martin Luther King and the Montgomery Story*, which sold for 10 cents in 1956. When Dr. King was murdered by an assassin's bullet in 1968, it felt to countless young people as if their Superman had died. In the days that followed his assassination in Memphis. Black communities mourned his death and publicly demonstrated against the injustice. Dr. King himself had said that riots were the language of the unheard, and this proved true in several American cities, including in Chicago; Detroit; Baltimore; Pittsburgh; Harlem, New York; Louisville, Kentucky; and elsewhere. As Black communities voiced their frustration, they were met with militarized force from local police as well as from the U.S. Army and the National Guard.

Robert F. Kennedy announced the assassination of Dr. Martin Luther King Jr. at a campaign rally on the evening of April 4, 1968, in Indianapolis, Indiana. Kennedy had learned of the assassination just hours prior and wanted to address the gathered community instead of canceling the engagement in its entirety. Historians often claim that Kennedy's speech should be credited with quelling the inevitable riot that would have happened among the Black community in Indiana, but in reality, the increased media coverage that resulted from his presence in Indianapolis may have been the only barrier stopping local police and the National Guard from descending on the Black community in the same way they did in other cities. On April 27, 1968, just weeks after her thirty-nine-year-old husband had been killed, human rights activist Coretta Scott King spoke at a rally in New York's Central Park, calling for peace in Vietnam and an end to the war. Alongside her children, Mrs. King dedicated her life to uplifting human rights efforts and shaping the legacy of Dr. King.

Believers in the Black Power movement would not allow it to be another dream deferred. At the 1968 Summer Olympics held in Mexico City, two young Black Olympic sprinters named John Carlos and Tommie Smith won the bronze and gold medals, respectively, for the two-hundred-meter race. Tommie Smith was born in 1944 in Texas and had moved to Southern California with his family like thousands of other Black families had during the Great Migration. While attending high school, he began to demonstrate a prowess for sprinting and eventually qualified for the Olympic team. John Carlos, born in 1945 in Harlem, was the son of Afro-Cuban parents and used his platform as an Olympian to advocate for human rights. Prior to participating in the 1968 Summer Olympics, Carlos and Smith had planned to boycott the event unless the four demands set by the Olympic Project for Human Rights were met. These demands called for the restoration of Muhammad Ali's heavyweight title, which had been stripped from him because of his opposition to the Vietnam War; the removal of the apartheid nations South Africa and Rhodesia from the Olympics; the inclusion of more Black coaches on the Olympic teams; and the removal of the International Olympic Committee president, who was a noted racist and anti-Semite.

The two athletes ultimately decided to participate in the Olympics, and upon becoming Olympic medalists, they took to the multileveled podium donning black socks without shoes, a reverent lowered gaze, and hands raised defiantly in the Black Power salute, while the national anthem sounded in the background. This live performance of political Blackness could not be censored and directly defied attempts by the International Olympic Committee to maintain an apolitical stance that did not interfere with the human rights abuses taking place in participating countries. Although Carlos and Smith were ultimately removed from the remaining Olympic Games for 1968 and barred from participating in any future Games, their defiant act drew international attention to the growing influence of the Black Power movement.

Black Power salute at the 1968 Summer Olympics

ALL POWER TO
ALL THE PEOPLE
1970—1979

BY 1970, MORE THAN HALF OF ALL BLACK AMERICANS RESIDED IN SOUTHERN STATES as compared to approximately 90 percent who had in 1910. This considerable internal migration did not just flow from south to north or north to west; it was also a rural to urban movement. By the time of the 1960 census, the impact of the Great Migration had an undeniable impact on urban cities. Whereas Alabama, Arkansas, Georgia, Louisiana, Mississippi, North Carolina, and South Carolina had each lost a hundred thousand or more individuals from Black communities, California, New York, Illinois, New Jersey, and Michigan each saw Black population growth in excess of a hundred thousand. Black people were still on the move.

In the 1970s, the Black American Great Migration officially ended, and the ten cities with the highest number of Black people were New York, Chicago,

Shirley Chisholm

Barbara Jordan

Detroit, Philadelphia, Los Angeles, Baltimore, Houston, Cleveland, New Orleans, and Washington, D.C. People from Jamaica, Puerto Rico, and elsewhere in the Caribbean also headed to U.S. cities during the 1960s and 1970s, often settling where the Black American community lived. While the waves of the Great Migration drew to a close during the 1970s, its impact did not suddenly stop once families settled in new cities. America was a land in transition. During the previous decade, the United States had sent men to the moon, and the technological age had ushered in handheld calculators and other advancements. However, as Black people, people of color, disabled folks, LGBTQ people, and women strived for equal footing, conservative groups likewise organized to curtail the momentum of human rights movements.

By the start of the 1970s, Black men were still being drafted at disproportionately high rates to serve in the war in Vietnam, Black Power organizations were still under surveillance by a wary government, and Black people were continuing to move to urban centers. In 1970, Carter G. Woodson created the weeklong celebration known as Negro History Week or Black History Week that was later expanded into the monthlong celebration of Black History Month. After pressure from activists and civil rights organizations, President Gerald Ford officially commemorated Black History Month as a symbolic attempt toward including Black Americans in the celebration of the two-hundred-year anniversary of the United States in 1976. Although Ford's intentions in recognizing a month dedicated to Black history may have been dubious, the designation was a welcome one for Black people, who had grown up as second-class citizens.

Although the promise of the Civil Rights movement had not yet been fulfilled, Black women political leaders like Shirley Chisholm and Barbara Jordan worked to transform the realm of politics. In the Bronx, DJ Kool Herc transformed music with the creation of hip-hop, and in Hollywood, Alex Haley brought previously untold elements of the Black American historical experience to mainstream audiences with the debut of the groundbreaking book and TV miniseries *Roots*. Throughout the 1970s, the Black community continued to thrive against the odds and continued to birth new avenues for creative expression.

In his 1970 spoken-word song "The Revolution Will Not Be Televised," Gil Scott-Heron poetically informed listeners that the revolution would not be manufactured or prepackaged but rather, as revealed in the last lyric of the song, the revolution would be live. Black students were able to enroll in colleges at historic rates during this period. Following the passage of the Civil Rights Act of 1964, Black enrollment in colleges and in secondary institutions nearly tripled from 250,000 to 750,000 just ten years later. By 1977, Black enrollment in colleges and universities exceeded 1,000,000, along with an increase in enrollment by other students of color, too. At colleges across the country, young people united and shared ideas about human rights and freedom. Momentum within the Antiwar movement, LGBTQ Rights movement, Women's Liberation movement, Indigenous Rights movement, Disability Rights movement, and the coalitions built among them transformed human rights in America through the power of the people.

A Black soldier in the Vietnam War

MAKE LOVE, NOT WAR

After decades of relative peacetime following World War II, the Vietnam War inspired young people to take to the streets to speak out against inequality in new ways. As their peers were being drafted, maimed, and killed in Vietnam, young people organized protests in opposition to U.S. involvement in the war. At one gathering of students on May 4, 1970, at Ohio's Kent State University, the Ohio National Guard opened fire and killed four students. Nine other students were injured, all while peacefully protesting the Vietnam War. At Jackson State University, a historically Black university, just eleven days later, more than forty Mississippi Highway Patrol officers fired over 150 shots at an occupied dormitory building, following an eruption of protests in response to a false report that Charles Evers, the son of civil rights legend Medgar Evers, had been murdered. Two students were killed, and twelve others were injured. National media covered the Kent State story and *Life* magazine dedicated its May 15, 1970, issue to the students who were killed there. Unlike Jackson State, Kent State was a predominantly white university, and the victims of the shooting were white themselves. The Jackson State shooting was only covered in Black media outlets, as if it had happened in a wholly different America.

Two years prior to these tragedies, at South Carolina State University, South Carolina Highway Patrol officers had fired into a gathered group of two hundred Black students who had been organizing for the integration of local recreation centers. In an act of retaliation against these young people who were pushing to upset the status quo, police killed university students Henry Smith and Samuel Hammond, as well as high school student Delano Middleton. In order to justify these extrajudicial killings and reckless acts, the police crafted a self-aggrandizing narrative, claiming that the protesters had been violent toward the police. The governor of South Carolina blamed the killing not on the unchecked racism within the police force but on the Black Power movement and unnamed "outside agitators" who must have antagonized the police. The same narrative repeats today, when police treat peaceful protestors with needless violence. Unlike the Kent State shootings that claimed the lives of white youth, the egregious act of police violence against Black students fell on unhearing ears. Today, the Kent State shooting sticks out in the public consciousness, while the shootings at the historically Black colleges Jackson State and South Carolina State University are remembered only by the survivors and their descendants.

Sylvia Rivera and Marsha P. Johnson

WE ARE EVERYWHERE

Just months before the dawn of the 1970s, during the evening hours of June 28, 1969, patrons at the Stonewall Inn on Christopher Street in Greenwich Village in Lower Manhattan rallied against the constant police surveillance and intimidation against their community. Over the following days, the LGBTQ community rose up against respectability, suppression, and police violence in what came to be known as the Stonewall Riots. The acts of resistance that took place at the Stonewall Inn inspired a new wave of LGBTQ activism in the 1970s. Black and Latinx transgender women like Marsha P. Johnson and Sylvia Rivera led the charge to transform the landscape of LGBTQ rights organizing and began working to advance the LGBTQ Rights movement. One year later, on June 28, 1970, the first Pride celebration was held in New York City.

LGBTQ people have been a part of American history since its inception, and leaders in the Black community, like Pauli Murray, Bayard Rustin, and James Baldwin, worked toward Black liberation, while they also worked toward LGBTQ liberation. One story from *Ebony* magazine that was originally published in 1951 discussed the story of Georgia Black, a Black transgender woman who lived and died in her truth. In 1975, during *Ebony* magazine's anniversary issue, Black's story was reprinted, and her name and identity were reborn in the public consciousness. In 2012, scholar Monica Roberts detailed (on her blog *Trans Griot*) Georgia Black's story in language that afforded the respect and dignity that she deserved, revealing that Black had been embraced by her community, faith group, and family. While initially written with sensationalist headlines, Black's story demonstrates that Black transgender women have always existed and that these stories are crucial to Black history and storytelling.

Prior to the Stonewall Riots and the ensuing years of activism, the popular sentiment in America toward LGBTQ people was one of transphobia and homophobia. In 1967, CBS reported that two out of three Americans looked upon homosexuals with "disgust, discomfort or fear." The American Psychiatric Association (APA) even considered homosexuality a mental illness through 1973. By the end of the decade, anti-LGBTQ legislation had been defeated in California, Minnesota, Oregon, Hawaii, Wisconsin, South Carolina, and elsewhere. In 1974, the APA unambiguously declared that homosexuality did not constitute a mental illness, and LGBTQ civil rights organizations were able to pass anti-discrimination legislation to protect LGBTQ people from being denied housing and employment.

WOMEN'S LIBERATION

The Women's Liberation movement fully emerged during the 1970s. Historically, this period of feminism is called second-wave feminism, following the first wave, which took place during the early twentieth century and focused on the issue of suffrage. At its core, the movement confronted the roles that women, men, and people of other genders were forced to conform to, although, like modern iterations of feminism, second wave feminism struggled to be inclusive when it came to race and class concerns. Women from various communities and movements, including the Black Power and Red Power movements, felt alienated by feminist leaders from white and middle-class backgrounds who rarely took feminist discourse beyond explorations of gender-based oppression. As social consciousness became more mainstream, feminist scholars were invited on television talk shows to make the case for gender equality. In one infamous instance, white tennis champions Billie Jean King, a woman, and Bobby Riggs, a man, were made to battle each other on air in what was billed as the Battle of the Sexes—the 1973 match became the most-watched sporting event of all time.

Despite the circus that played out on television, the Women's Liberation movement raised consciousness about the many causes on the line. The right to end a pregnancy, or have an abortion, was denied in over thirty states at the dawn of the 1970s. With the U.S. Supreme Court decision made in *Roe v. Wade* (1973), the right to end a pregnancy and ultimately control one's own reproductive health was secured, though it continues to be threatened on the state and local levels.

Black women had been largely sidelined in the movement for civil rights. As demonstrated during the 1963 March on Washington, straight Black men dominated the majority of the programming, with Black women providing entertainment and giving a brief speech on the contributions made by women in the Civil Rights movement. Black women were forced to simultaneously fight against white supremacy and patriarchy within movements that failed to account for their existence. Just as the Women's Liberation movement confronted the role of women in society and the Black Power movement explored the position Black people held, Black queer women like Audre Lorde and Angela Davis gained prominence, as they negotiated the intersections of their identities. Lorde, a Black lesbian poet and feminist scholar, taught students about the intersectional identity of Black women and created the foundation of Black queer feminist theory. In 1973, Lorde published *From a Land Where Other People Live*, a collection of poetry that discussed the second-class status endured by Black queer women. By the 1970s, Black lesbian activist Angela Davis was a household name for her work opposing war, racism, sexism, and incarceration. In 1969, California governor

Ronald Reagan attempted to ban Davis from teaching in California because of her participation in the Communist Party. One year later, Davis was arrested for her alleged role in trying to liberate prisoners from a courtroom in California and came to represent the ways in which Black women are policed and brutalized in a system of patriarchy and white supremacy.

The dual forces of the Women's Liberation movement and the Black Power movement also made a path for Shirley Chisholm and Barbara Jordan to enter the political sphere as trailblazers securing many firsts. Chisholm was born in Brooklyn, although her parents had immigrated from the Caribbean. In 1968, Chisholm became the first Black woman elected to the U.S. Congress, where she served consecutive terms until 1983. In 1972, she also became the first Black and woman candidate of either of the two major parties to run for president of the United States. Jordan, raised in Texas, had family roots elsewhere in the South, but her family, like so many others, decided to stay in the South and work toward its betterment. In Texas, on March 28, 1972, Jordan, then serving as a member of the Texas Senate, was elected by her fellow legislators as president pro tempore. One of her responsibilities in this elevated role was to become acting governor of the state if the elected governor and lieutenant governor were to travel outside the state simultaneously—which happened on June 10, 1972. Even though her governorship was due to a technicality, it made Jordan the first Black woman governor of a U.S. state (like P. B. S. Pinchback before her). In 1976, Jordan also became the first Black woman to provide the keynote address at a Democratic National Convention. Women, and Black women in particular, were changing the face of American democracy.

THE RED POWER MOVEMENT

In the 1960s and 1970s, the Red Power movement, or Indigenous Rights movement, brought about a transformation in the rights of Native Americans, who had only been granted U.S. citizenship in 1924. Inspired by the Black Power movement, the Red Power movement focused on the establishment of cultural, political, and social institutions created by and for the Native American community. Like Black people, Native Americans were also denied the right to vote because of barriers imposed by poll taxes, vigilantism, and literacy tests until the passage of the Voting Rights Act of 1965. Instead of providing dedicated resources to Native American communities, the U.S. Congress passed the Indian Relocation Act of 1956, which, as part of a larger Indian termination policy, encouraged Native Americans to move from reservations to urban areas, with the ultimate goal of assimilating Native people into Eurocentric American society. In response to these policies, which included the forced relocation, reeducation, and termination of tribal designations, young people began to organize acts of civil disobedience to raise awareness of the injustices faced by Native Americans.

On November 20, 1969, eighty-nine Native American organizers with the support of Indians of All Tribes led the reoccupation of Alcatraz Island, which until 1963 had been a federal penitentiary. Alcatraz is an island in the San Francisco Bay Area, a region that was a haven for the counterculture and antiwar movements of the era. The reoccupation of Alcatraz was a demonstration aimed at reclaiming the stolen land that comprises America and creating awareness about the resources denied and injustices thrust upon Native Americans. In 1969, Native American organizer Richard Oakes issued the Alcatraz Proclamation to the San Francisco Department of the Interior to assert the demands of the movement. The proclamation outlined the similarities between Alcatraz Island and Indian reservations. Importantly, the proclamation referred to the historical indignities suffered by Native Americans, including the forced assimilation, reeducation, and colonization at the hands of the U.S. government. In 1971, after nineteen months of occupation and protest, the people occupying Alcatraz Island were forcibly removed from the land. The movement was successful in drawing international attention to the oppression of Native Americans.

In the years following the occupation of Alcatraz Island, other acts of civil disobedience by Native American people spread across the United States. In 1973, two hundred Oglala Lakota tribal members alongside followers of the American Indian Movement (AIM) reoccupied the city of Wounded Knee, South Dakota, where three hundred members of the Lakota tribe had been massacred by U.S. forces in 1890. Law enforcement and the Federal Bureau of Investigation forced the tribal members off the land after seventy-one days of occupation that claimed the lives of two Sioux men who were killed by federal agents.

Stevie Wonder and
Marvin Gaye record a
song together at the
Motown Records studio
in Detroit, Michigan.

Native American organizers had many injustices to fight against. Lobbying by organizers within AIM resulted in the 1978 passage of the Indian Child Welfare Act. Before the passage of this act, Native American parents were forced to enroll their children in boarding schools aimed at indoctrinating Native American children with European and Christian ideologies, but in 1978, parents were finally given the legal right to opt out of this harmful program. However, the generational trauma caused by these programs and the lasting effects of Native American colonization and erasure continue today.

THE FUTURE IS ACCESSIBLE

Despite the progress that had been made during the Civil Rights and other progressive movements in the 1950s, '60s, and early '70s, disabled people were largely left out of the conversation. Throughout the 1900s, disabled people of all races were marginalized. The majority of advancements made by the disabled community came from advocacy by disabled veterans from World War II and the Korean War. After limited progress, in April of 1977, the landscape for disability rights organizing was on the precipice of a revolution. During the twentieth century, the forced sterilization of people with disabilities was upheld by the courts and implemented nationwide. These indignities continued unchecked, because there was no civil rights legislation that protected people with disabilities.

Community organizations worked to provide for disabled Americans; in Oakland, California, a disabled Black Panther member named Bradley Lomax was working to provide a community-based solution to disability outreach, because other infrastructure failed to include poor people and people of color. Disability rights organizers worked to resolve the lack of protections by lobbying Joseph Califano, U.S. Secretary of Health, Education, and Welfare, to include regulations that would allow disabled Americans to receive the crucial protections listed in Section 504 of the Rehabilitation Act of 1973, which ensured that disabled people would not be subjected to discrimination on the basis of disability. After Califano refused to respond to warnings of protests on April 5, 1977, disability rights activists implemented the successful tactics of the Civil Rights movement and peacefully occupied the offices of the U.S. Department of Health, Education, and Welfare through sit-ins in Atlanta, Boston, Chicago, Denver, Los Angeles, New York, Philadelphia, San Francisco, Seattle, and Washington, D.C. In San Francisco, Lomax enlisted the support of the Black Panther Party to provide the food that allowed the protesters to occupy the building for twenty-five days. Additional pressure created by the 504 sit-ins pushed Califano to issue regulations that would finally result in the enforcement of Section 504.

Modern-day disability rights activist Vilissa Thompson notes that the crucial role of the Black Panther Party in making the protest successful had been minimized and even erased within the broader disability rights community. Without the infrastructure and coalition building across movement groups, the 1970s would not have been remembered for so many historic wins. Black American children's advocate Marian Wright Edelman founded the Children's Defense Fund (CDF) in 1973 to continue the mission of the Civil Rights movement for the benefit of children. Her work within the CDF brought improvements to children's education and helped pass the Education for All Handicapped Children Act in 1975. In 1978, disability rights advocates also organized to require public transportation to be accessible for wheelchairs. The protests inspired the formation of ADAPT and led to the creation and signing of the Americans with Disabilities Act twenty years later in 1990.

THE SOUL OF A NATION

In 1969, Norman Whitfield wrote an antiwar ballad simply named "War," with the Temptations recording the initial version for their album. Fearing that such a clear antiwar message could tarnish the sterling image of the straight-laced Temptations, who were better known for love songs like "My Girl" (1965), Motown Records founder Berry Gordy decided to rerelease the song as a single with a new artist named Edwin Starr. Adding in more theatrical intensity, James Brown–esque shouts and ad libs, and the horns and drums characteristic to soul music, Starr's cover of "War" (1970) became an instant hit among young people protesting against the war in Vietnam. The growing unrest in America was also felt by popular artists at the time, including Marvin Gaye, who released the protest song "What's Going On" (1971), and Stevie Wonder, who released myriad ballads on topics ranging from poverty to war in songs like "Living for the City" (1973) and "Front Line" (1983).

As television took an increasingly prominent role in the lives of Americans, *Soul Train*, a music and dance show hosted by Don Cornelius that he started in 1971, provided a weekly view into the world of Black American culture. Every Saturday, young people in cities across the country would tune in to *Soul Train* to see the popular dances that would dominate dance floors each week. With no DVRs to record the show and replay at a later time, groups of young people

Don Cornelius

would assemble in their parents' living rooms to memorize the new dances as they flashed across the screen. *Soul Train* provided young people from different communities and different cities with a common culture, as the show introduced American teens to new dance moves, apparel, and musical groups. Some of the first dancers who appeared on *Soul Train* spotted Don Cornelius's advertisement for dancers in *The Chicago Defender*, a newspaper that had been central to showcasing opportunities for Black people living in the South during the Great Migration. Prior to being broadcast nationally, *Soul Train* aired in cities with large Black communities, including Detroit, Chicago, Philadelphia, and Los Angeles—all of which owed their vast communities to the internal migration that had occurred in the previous decades.

In 1977, American audiences were introduced to the groundbreaking TV mini-series *Roots*, based on Alex Haley's 1976 novel of the same name. *Roots* was unlike anything most Americans had ever seen in that it followed the life of Kunta Kinte (portrayed by LeVar Burton)—an African man who was captured, sold into slavery, and transported to America—and his descendants, right down to Haley himself. *Roots* forced America to confront the unspoken chapters of American history. Before *Roots*, enslaved people were portrayed as jovial participants in the horrific institution of slavery and not as survivors of human brutality. At a time when there were only four television channels, ABC broadcast *Roots* into the homes of Americans and aired it over eight consecutive nights instead of weekly to minimize the advertising loss the network expected the show to create. Executives at the network anticipated that few white Americans would tune in to the show and ultimately expected it to fail; however, more than 40 percent of all American homes watched the first episode of the series compared to a projected viewership of 28 percent. The show became a cultural force and inspired many in the Black community to research their own connections to the African continent. The series also cast popular actors from prime-time shows such as John Amos from *Good Times*, Robert Reed from *The Brady Bunch*, and Richard Roundtree from the film *Shaft* to make cameo appearances. *Roots* provided a historically accurate glimpse into the lives of everyday Black families who had survived enslavement and crucially centered those families in the process.

"I SAID A HIP HOP"

Hip-hop, perhaps the most important musical genre in contemporary culture, emerged during the 1970s, in large part because of the Great Migration. Without the massive internal migration of over six million Black people, there would not have been the swell of Black people living in the urban areas that came to define the genre. Across the Harlem River in the New York City borough of the Bronx, the migrations of Black southerners, Puerto Ricans, and people from the Caribbean coalesced into a vibrant and diverse urban community that created a new world culture while simultaneously retaining their own. Starting during World War II, Puerto Ricans, Cubans, Panamanians, Dominicans, and other Spanish-speaking communities formed barrios across New York in the Bronx, Brooklyn, and areas of Harlem. During the 1960s, Jamaicans and Haitians had continued immigrating to Los Angeles, Chicago, Atlanta, Miami, and New York, settling in the same urban centers as the Black American southerners of the Great Migration. Although these communities spoke many languages—Spanish, French, African American English, jive, and patois—they all spoke the language of music. In the Bronx, Black, Jamaican, Puerto Rican, and Cuban young people collaborated, giving rise to the four elements of a new genre called hip-hop. Although the term to describe this new form of music was a few years off, hip-hop officially began with a back-to-school party organized by DJ Kool Herc in the recreation room of 1520 Sedgwick Avenue in Harlem on August 11, 1973.

In 1979, "I said a hip hop" were the first words on the Sugarhill Gang's song "Rapper's Delight." The song became a mainstay among children, teens, and young adults of color, who eagerly learned the song's edgy lyrics. The historical use of the words "hip" and "hop" had existed in Black culture well before the 1970s. Black folks had been using the term "hop" in reference to dance since the 1920s, when famous Black dancers popularized the Lindy Hop during the Harlem Renaissance. The term "hip" had long been used to refer to something innovative, and in the 1960s, "Are you hip?" was a common question among young people to inquire about a person's cultural and social awareness. The new musical style relied on four parts brought together by the waves of the Great Migration, which united Black and Latinx people in urban, industrial centers, frequently in the

TIME

WHY 'ROOTS' HIT HOME

Alex Haley

Cover of *Time*, February 14, 1977

DJ Kool Herc

same public housing accommodations and neighborhoods. These four elements included: movement and break dancing, or "b-boying"; music, or "djing"; street art and style, or graffiti; and rapping, or "mc'ing."

Hip-hop was among the counterculture movements of the 1970s that included rock music, communal living, antiwar organizing, and Black power. Hip-hop sought to reject the marginalization of Black and Latinx communities in New York and promoted unity and strength in the midst of the devastation created by President Richard Nixon's war on drugs, which continued into the Reagan era in the 1980s. The war on drugs increased the number of people incarcerated for nonviolent drug offenses from fifty thousand in 1980 to more than four hundred thousand by 1997 and primarily targeted the Black and Latinx communities. Amid the rise of police violence and mass incarceration, artist Afrika Bambaataa declared knowledge as the fifth element of hip-hop, indicative of its importance as a movement of social commentary. In this way, hip-hop gave voice to a new generation in many of the same ways that blues, jazz, and soul had done for Black people in the past. As inequalities and injustices against Black Americans grew, so did the genre that told their stories.

Invitation to DJ Kool Herc's Back to School Jam party, 1973

CONCLUSION

I am the granddaughter of people who survived Jim Crow racism and moved from Arkansas and Louisiana to California during the Great Migration. As a Black person of mixed heritage, I am the descendant of people who were enslaved as well as people who owned slaves. Researching and writing this book has helped me understand myself, my own family, and Black American identity, and I hope it does the same for you.

When I was a child, I was fortunate to spend a lot of time with my grand-mother Verna Jean, whom I call Mama Brown. Many of her stories inspired me to write this book. On October 16, 2018, I visited Mama Brown to interview her about her childhood—it was just months before her ninetieth birthday and the very same day that my first book *Modern HERstory* was published. It was a tearful reunion, filled with memories and iPhone photo album reviews. When we had caught up on family affairs and there was a lull in the conversation, she turned to me and began to tell me about the first time she had gone to a movie theater and realized she had to sit in the segregated balcony. Tears filled her eyes upon the recollection. At ninety years old, Mama Brown had lived a quintessentially American life, although as a Black woman born in 1928, her story was one of survival. She had lived through and survived many of the events that I can only read about.

My grandmother was born in Arkansas, the cradle of Jim Crow racism. At the age of six, she witnessed the lynching of Willie Kees, and her family was forced to move out West to avoid the racist violence of the Ku Klux Klan (KKK). She told me about the sudden removal of her Japanese American classmates in California in the weeks following the bombing of Pearl Harbor. She witnessed the rise of Dr. Martin Luther King Jr.—she was just a month older than he was—and she experienced his assassination just weeks before her youngest child turned eighteen. She lived through the Women's Liberation movement, read about the Stonewall Riots in the newspaper, and watched Neil Armstrong walk on the moon on a black-and-white television set. When Senator Barack Obama announced his candidacy for president, she joked with me that she would personally hold a parade if he won— which he did. She was thrilled to witness Barack Obama's inauguration as our first Black president and experienced the gut-wrenching election of the forty-fifth president, who intended to make the United States return to the frightening reality of her childhood. Verna Jean has lived an American life.

In California, members of my family reacted in differing ways to the assassinations of Medgar Evers, El Hajj Malik El Shabazz (also known as Malcolm X), Dr. Martin Luther King Jr., and Robert F. Kennedy. My father,

DeWalt, who was eighteen and college bound in 1968, began preparing himself for the world of business, where he hoped to excel economically and improve the conditions of his community through financial gain. He also felt compelled to explore the reemerging Pan-African movement and joined Operation Crossroads Africa, traveling to Ethiopia and Kenya, where he taught children in local communities about clean water practices and ultimately reconnected with his roots.

My uncle Vernon was nineteen in 1968 and had decided to forego the traditional academic path to study carpentry like his father. After high school, Vernon joined the Los Angeles chapter of the Black Panther Party and worked to build up community-created infrastructure in a country that had so clearly abandoned Black people. In 1969, when the Chicago police executed Fred Hampton, who was then chairman of the Illinois Black Panther Party, Vernon fled to Jamaica out of fear that the Los Angeles chapter could be similarly targeted. Before he passed, Uncle Vernon gave me glimpses of his youth activism but largely kept this chapter of his life private because of the pain it reanimated.

My uncle Craig became politically active and led the Altadena, California, office for Democratic hopeful Eugene McCarthy. In 1968, Craig went to the

Chicago Democratic Convention, where, even though he was working on the "Be Clean for Gene" campaign, he was teargassed because he was perceived to be part of the protest groups. Such was the hazard of being Black during the 1960s. This incident inspired him to work inside the system, and he became a police officer in Oakland, California. In one state, and even within one family, young people responded very differently to the chaos of 1968, and they prepared themselves to enter into a new decade.

The story of America is an incomplete one if it does not include those who have been pushed to the margins. Much of Black American history has been passed down in the oral tradition or lost to time. We are a diverse and multifaceted people, stolen from our roots and surviving on stolen land. I have done my part in that history telling with *Making Our Way Home: The Great Migration and the Black American Dream* and I hope you feel inspired to look to your own family and learn about your own history.

GLOSSARY

16TH STREET BAPTIST CHURCH BOMBING (1963): On September 15, 1963, members of the Ku Klux Klan (KKK), a racist hate group, committed an act of domestic terrorism with the bombing of the 16th Street Baptist Church in Birmingham, Alabama. The bombing resulted in the deaths of four young Black American girls and the injury of over twenty additional parishioners. The four victims included eleven-year-old Carol Denise McNair and fourteen-year-olds Addie Mae Collins, Carole Robertson, and Cynthia Wesley.

504 SIT-INS (1977): A series of disability rights protests organized by disabled organizers that began on April 5, 1977. The protests successfully pressured the U.S. Department of Health, Education, and Welfare to create regulations concerning the enforcement of Section 504 of the Rehabilitation Act of 1973.

A. PHILIP RANDOLPH (1889–1979): A leader in the Civil Rights movement who made vast contributions to the Labor movement. In 1925, Randolph's efforts led to the founding of the Brotherhood of Sleeping Car Porters, the first predominantly Black labor union. In 1963, Randolph and Bayard Rustin became the architects of the March on Washington, which is remembered for Dr. Martin Luther King Jr.'s "I Have a Dream" speech.

ABORTION: The term "abortion" refers to the ending of a pregnancy.

ABRAHAM LINCOLN (1809–1865): America's 16th president, Lincoln led the United States through the Civil War, its bloodiest war and its greatest moral, constitutional, and political crisis at the time. He was the first president to be assassinated in 1865.

ADAPT: Founded in Denver, Colorado, in 1974 as the Atlantis Community, ADAPT is a national grass-roots community that organizes disability rights activists to engage in nonviolent direct action, including civil disobedience, to ensure the civil and human rights of disabled people to live in freedom.

ADOLF HITLER (1889–1945): An anti-Semitic Nazi political leader from Austria–Hungary, Adolf Hitler was responsible for the genocide, starvation, torture, and slaughter of more than seventeen million people, including six million Jewish people, across Europe during the Holocaust, or Shoah, that lasted from 1941 to 1945. Hitler systematically targeted Jewish people in addition to Roma people, Croatian people, Bosnian and Herzegovinian people, LGBTQ people, disabled people, political dissidents, Soviet civilians, Polish people, and individuals living at the intersections of these many groups.

AFRICAN AMERICAN ENGLISH (AAE): A dialect of American English, also known as Black American English, AAE was created and used by Black people in the United States. It has its own grammatical structure and terminology that can differ among the various regions where it is used.

AFRICAN METHODIST EPISCOPAL CHURCH: The first independent Protestant denomination to be founded by Black people in 1816 (it's also called the A.M.E. Church or AME). The church was instrumental in settling Black people during the Great Migration and in providing job skills and literacy programs to congregation and community members.

AFRIKA BAMBAATAA (1957–): A Black American disc jockey and activist of Barbadian and Jamaican ancestry, Afrika Bambaataa is a major figure in the creation of hip-hop and is often referred to as the genre's godfather. As a DJ, Bambaataa popularized hip-hop culture in the 1980s and later created a musical style that combined electronica and funk.

AFRO: In the United States, "afro" is a term that gained prominence following the 1950s to describe the natural hairstyle of Black and African diasporic peoples. During the Black is Beautiful movement in the 1960s, an afro became a symbol of social consciousness, because it emphasized the beauty in natural hair instead of more mainstream beliefs that Black hair had to be chemically treated or processed to be desirable. The afro is characterized by tight curls brushed or picked to resemble a spherical halo.

ALAIN LOCKE (1885–1954): A Black American philosopher, scholar, and educator. In 1907, Locke became the first Black American Rhodes Scholar and provided much of the philosophy for the Harlem Renaissance with his book *The New Negro* (1925).

ALEX HALEY (1921–1992): A Black American historian and author of the 1976 book *Roots: The Saga of an American Family*. In 1977, a television miniseries of the same name that was adapted from his book aired on ABC, fundamentally changing the way that Black history was told in popular culture.

AMERICAN: A term that can refer to people from or living in any country in North, Central, or South America in addition to the Caribbean and other islands surrounding the American continents. For the purposes of this book and for brevity, American will refer to people residing in the United States.

AMERICAN INDIAN MOVEMENT (AIM): A Native American advocacy group in the United States, AIM was founded in July 1968 in Minneapolis.

AMOS HALL (1892–1971): Born in Louisiana, Hall was a Black American lawyer and one of the most significant civil rights lawyers in the state of Oklahoma. Hall represented Black teachers, community members, and young people, winning several cases, including *Freeman v. Oklahoma City School Board* (1948).

ANDREW CARNEGIE (1835–1919): A Scottish-born white American industrialist, Carnegie was known for leading the steel industry into the nineteenth century. As a philanthropist, he supported the National Negro Business League and funded separate libraries for Black people instead of creating integrated ones.

ANGELA DAVIS (1944–): A Black American lesbian political activist, scholar, and author from Birmingham, Alabama. She is known for her advocacy against oppression globally and is the author of many books, including *Women, Race and Class* (1981), *Angela Davis: An Autobiography* (1974), and *Freedom Is a Constant Struggle* (2015).

ANNIE TURNBO MALONE (1877–1957): A Black American entrepreneur, inventor, and philanthropist alongside Madam C. J. Walker, Malone became one of the first Black women millionaires in the United States. She mentored Walker, and the two worked closely together in the hair care and cosmetics industries.

ANTI-BLACK: A person or an entity that is opposed to, hostile toward, or antagonistic to Black people or the culture, values, and interests of the Black community.

ANTI-SEMITIC: A person or an entity that participates in the prejudiced treatment, stereotyping, targeting, oppression, or discrimination of Jewish people.

AUDRE LORDE (1934–1992): A Black lesbian American writer, womanist, and human rights activist from Harlem, New York. She was recognized for her poetry, scholarship, and works such as *Sister Outsider* (1984), *Zami* (1982), and *From a Land Where Other People Live* (1973).

BARACK HUSSEIN OBAMA (1961–): A Black American politician and the 44th president of the United States, who served from 2009 to 2017. He is the first Black American president in U.S. history. Following his presidency, he established the Obama Foundation to inspire and empower young leaders and civic innovators to change their world. He is married to Michelle Obama.

BARBARA JORDAN (1936–1996): A Black lesbian American lawyer and politician who won a seat in the Texas Senate in 1966. On June 10, 1972, although through a technicality, she became the first Black woman governor of a U.S. state, serving as the acting governor because of her position as president pro tempore of the Texas Senate.

BAYARD RUSTIN (1912–1987): An openly gay Black American civil rights leader, Rustin was instrumental in the creation and implementation of countless programs of the Civil Rights movement. While he is often cited as a civil rights leader, his identity as a gay man is often erased. Rustin supported the formation of the Congress of Racial Equality (CORE), was an architect of the March on Washington (1963), and was an organizer of the Freedom Rides (1961).

BENJAMIN O. DAVIS JR. (1912–2002): A Black American U.S. Air Force general and commander of the World War II Tuskegee Airmen, Davis was the first Black American general in the U.S. Air Force.

BERRY GORDY (1929–): A Black American entrepreneur, producer, and songwriter. He founded Motown Records in 1959. For decades, Motown was the highest-earning Black-owned business in the United States.

BESSIE SMITH (1894–1937): A Black American blues singer and dancer who gained prominence during the Harlem Renaissance in the 1920s and 1930s for her vivacious performances, earning her the title of Empress of the Blues.

BLACK HISTORY MONTH: Established in 1970 by President Gerald Ford after decades of advocacy by civil rights organizations, Black History Month is an annual celebration of Black history during the month of February. *See also* **Black History Week**.

BLACK HISTORY WEEK: First called Negro History Week, Black History Week (BHW) was a weeklong celebration of Black history during the second week of February. BHW was the precursor to Black History Month, and was created in 1926 by Black American historian Carter G. Woodson. The timing of the celebration was chosen because it coincided with the birthdays of Abraham Lincoln on February 12 and of Frederick Douglass on February 14.

BLACK IS BEAUTIFUL: A movement that emerged out of the Black Power movement and permeated popular culture, beauty, and fashion during the 1960s and 1970s. The movement replaced the internalized notion of inferiority (which had been perpetuated by segregation and discrimination) with empowerment.

BLACK PANTHER PARTY FOR SELF-DEFENSE: An organization (also known as the Black Panther Party) founded by Huey Newton and Bobby Seale, in October 1966 in Oakland, California. Initially, the organization was a community-based solution to police and vigilante violence against the Black community. The Black Panther Party had national chapters that carried out free food programs, free medical care programs, and more. After years of harassment and surveillance by law enforcement, including the FBI, the Black Panther Party officially dissolved in 1982. Members of the Black Panther Party included Kwame Ture, Elaine Brown, and Kathleen Cleaver.

BLACK POWER: While the phrase Black Power gained popularity following a 1966 speech by Trinidadian activist Kwame Ture, who was the president of the Student Nonviolent Coordinating Committee (SNCC), the earliest use of the phrase was in Richard Wright's 1954 book *Black Power*. The ideology of Black Power focused on the establishment of cultural, political, and social institutions that uplifted and promoted the needs and interests of the Black community. Black Power is rooted in Pan-Africanism and Garveyism.

BLACK POWER SALUTE (1968 MEXICO CITY SUMMER OLYMPICS): During the 1968 Olympics, John Carlos and Tommie Smith, who had won the bronze and gold medals, respectively, in the two-hundred-meter race, took to the multileveled Olympic podium donning black socks without shoes, a reverent lowered gaze, and hands raised defiantly in the Black Power salute, as the national anthem sounded in the background. Their act of resistance against the Olympic institution, which had allowed apartheid nations to participate and had a racist anti-Semite as the International Olympic Committee president, resulted in the ousting of Carlos and Smith from the Games.

BLIND LEMON JEFFERSON (1893–1929): A Black blind American blues and gospel singer, songwriter, and musician from Texas, Jefferson is remembered as the godfather of Texas blues.

BLUE DISCHARGE: Also known as a blue ticket, blue discharge was a form of administrative military discharge that became common practice in the U.S. military, starting in 1916 and continuing into 1949. Blue discharges were disproportionately issued to LGBTQ and Black servicemen. Between 1941 and 1945, the U.S. Army issued approximately 22 percent of the more than 48,000 blue discharge papers to Black soldiers, who constituted less than 7 percent of the army.

BOBBY SEALE (1936–): Bobby Seale was a Black American political activist and cofounder of the Black Panther Party. He worked alongside Huey Newton to create the Black Panther Party's Ten-Point Platform as the strategic map for the organization and for the Black community. Seale's autobiography *A Lonely Rage* (1988) provides a firsthand account of Black Power organizing.

BOOKER T. WASHINGTON (1856–1915): A Black American scholar and advisor to leaders of the United States, Washington founded the Tuskegee Institute, a university in Tuskegee, Alabama, and also founded the National Negro Business League (NNBL) to centralize Black business leaders and accelerate the economic growth of the Black community.

BOYNTON V. VIRGINIA (1960): Bruce Boynton, a Black American law student, was charged with trespassing after he entered a segregated restaurant in a Richmond, Virginia, bus station and sat on the side reserved for white customers. The case made its way to the U.S. Supreme Court, and in 1960, the court overturned the conviction on the basis that racial segregation on public interstate transportation violated the Interstate Commerce Act, which prohibited discrimination in interstate passenger transportation.

BRADLEY LOMAX (YEARS UNKNOWN): A disabled Black American activist and Black Panther member, Lomax formed coalitions between the Disability Rights movement and the Black Power movement. His work helped secure food and resources that allowed the 504 sit-ins to continue for twenty-five days and successfully pressure the enforcement of Section 504 of the Rehabilitation Act of 1973, which gave much-needed protections to disabled Americans.

BROTHERHOOD OF SLEEPING CAR PORTERS: The first labor organization led by Black people to receive a charter in the American Federation of Labor.

BROWN V. BOARD OF EDUCATION (1954):
Thurgood Marshall argued in the *Brown v. Board of Education* case that the Topeka, Kansas, Board of Education was denying students their constitutional right to equal protection as guaranteed by the Fourteenth Amendment, and on May 17, 1954, the all-white panel of U.S. Supreme Court judges unanimously decided to overturn the *Plessy v. Ferguson* (1896) "separate but equal" doctrine. The ruling in *Brown v. Board of Education* simply ordered state attorneys general to integrate American schools "with all deliberate speed" but did not provide any means of enforcement or accountability.

CARTER G. WOODSON (1875–1950): A Black American historian, author, and journalist who founded the Association for the Study of African American Life and History in 1915. In addition to pioneering the study of Black American history, he established Negro History Week in 1926 (which later became Black History Month).

CATHERINE BURKS (1939–): A Black American civil rights activist and educator. She participated in the 1961 Freedom Rides from Nashville, Tennessee, to Montgomery, Alabama, and participated in Fannie Lou Hamer's Freedom Summer program for voter registration.

CESAR CHAVEZ (1927–1993): A Mexican American civil rights activist and labor organizer who cofounded the United Farm Workers of America in 1962, alongside Dolores Huerta, Larry Itliong, and Philip Vera Cruz.

CHATTEL SLAVERY: The type of enslavement suffered by millions of Africans and their descendants from the 1520s through the 1860s. Under this form of slavery, enslaved Africans were treated as property or "chattel" to be bought, sold, traded, or inherited. It was unique in that enslavement was passed down matriarchally, meaning that an enslaved woman's children were also enslaved.

CHILDREN'S DEFENSE FUND: A nonprofit organization in the United States founded in 1973 by Marian Wright Edelman that focuses on child advocacy and research.

CHUCK BERRY (1926–2017): A Black American singer and songwriter born in St. Louis, Missouri. With hit songs like "Rock and Roll Music" (1957) and "Johnny B. Goode" (1958), Berry became a prominent pioneer of rock 'n' roll.

CIVIL RIGHTS ACT OF 1875: Legislation signed into law by President Ulysses S. Grant during Reconstruction that protected the civil rights of Black American men by prohibiting discrimination in jury selection and voting. Enforcement of the act was not effective and Black men seeking to exercise their civil rights were victims of vigilante violence by hate groups.

CIVIL RIGHTS MOVEMENT: The collective efforts of leaders and groups from 1954 to 1968 aimed toward ending racial segregation, race- and class-based discrimination, and protecting the civil and human rights of marginalized Americans in the United States. Leaders of the Civil Rights movement utilized direct action strategies, legal procedure, and media to advocate for change.

CIVIL WAR (1861–1865): After years of resentment between the Northern and Southern American states, the issue of slavery and the economic advantages it provided in the South launched the United States into a civil war. The South separated or seceded from the North, which, during the war, was called the Union, and established a government called the Confederacy. In all, 620,000 people died during the Civil War, and the Union won.

CLAUDE MCKAY (1889–1948): A Jamaican American writer and poet who gained prominence during the Harlem Renaissance. McKay never came out during his lifetime, although his sexual orientation is often interpreted as gay or bisexual by LGBTQ history scholars because his works reveal queer relationships. Some of McKay's works include *If We Must Die* (1919), *The Lynching* (1922), and *America* (1921).

COINTELPRO: Established in 1956 by J. Edgar Hoover, the FBI's Counterintelligence Program, better known as COINTELPRO, aimed to gather intelligence on and destabilize Black civil rights and communist organizations, often through illegal means.

COLD WAR: The name given to the open political hostility between the United States and the Soviet Union from 1945 to 1990.

COLORISM: Refers to the prejudice that favors a lighter skin color, or a perceived proximity to whiteness, within and among communities, cultures, and groups.

CONFEDERACY: *See* **Confederate States of America.**

CONFEDERATE STATES OF AMERICA: A failed and unrecognized state that seceded from the United States in 1861 over the issue of enslavement. The seceded states included Alabama, Arkansas, Florida, Georgia, Mississippi, North Carolina, South Carolina, Tennessee, Texas, and Virginia. In 1865, the Confederacy dissolved, following its defeat in the Civil War.

CONGRESS OF RACIAL EQUALITY (CORE): James Farmer, Bayard Rustin, George Houser, and Bernice Fisher founded CORE in Chicago in 1942 to mobilize for racial equality.

CONSCIENTIOUS OBJECTOR: In the United States, a conscientious objector is a person who has "firm, fixed, and sincere objection to participation in war in any form or the bearing of arms, by reason of religious training and/or belief."

CORETTA SCOTT KING (1927–2006): A Black American author, civil rights leader, and the wife of Dr. Martin Luther King Jr. who was an active advocate for equality and helped lead the Civil Rights movement during the 1960s.

CORNELIUS JOHNSON (1913–1946): A Black American Olympic gold medalist who competed during the 1936 Berlin Summer Olympics. Like Jesse Owens, Johnson was also met with discrimination upon his return to the United States, where he was not formally recognized or acknowledged for his accomplishments.

COUNTEE CULLEN (1903–1946): A Black American poet who gained recognition during the Harlem Renaissance. While he never came out during his lifetime, he did write to Alain Locke about finding inspiration in gay-affirming texts and was a prominent figure within LGBTQ circles of the Harlem Renaissance. Some of Cullen's works include *Copper Sun* (1927), *The Black Christ* (1929), and *Any Human to Another* (1934).

THE CRISIS: W. E. B. Du Bois founded *The Crisis*, the official magazine of the National Association for the Advancement of Colored People (NAACP), in 1910. The magazine helped inform Black Americans across the United States about the efforts of the NAACP and other civil rights organizations to dismantle racist institutions.

DIANA ROSS (1944–): A Black American singer, actor, and producer who rose to prominence during the 1960s with the success of the Supremes, the Motown group of which she was the lead singer. After becoming a solo artist in 1970, she continued her career in singing as well as acting, winning many awards in recognition of her talents.

DIANE NASH (1938–): A Black American leader and strategist during the Civil Rights movement, Nash bravely continued the Freedom Rides even after violence from opposition groups. Nash also participated in the integration of lunch counters, the Student Nonviolent Coordinating Committee (SNCC), and the Freedom Summer project.

DISABILITY RIGHTS MOVEMENT: This ongoing movement of activists, leaders, and organizations works toward the goal of ending ableism and promotes the civil and human rights of disabled people globally.

DJ KOOL HERC (1955–): Also known as Clive "DJ Kool Herc" Campbell, Herc is a Jamaican American disc jockey who is credited with giving rise to the music genre of hip-hop in the 1970s in the Bronx, New York City.

DOLORES HUERTA (1930–): A Mexican American civil rights and labor organizing activist, Huerta founded the Agricultural Workers Association in 1960 and went on to become a cofounder of the United Farm Workers Association in 1962.

DOMESTIC TERRORISM: A term that describes terror that is carried out by groups within a state with the goal of committing violence against or intimidating civilians to influence or coerce government policy through organized destruction such as assassination and threats of force.

DON CORNELIUS (1936–2012): A Black American television producer and show host who created *Soul Train*, a nationally syndicated dance and music program that aired from 1971 until 1993. In each episode, Cornelius would sign off: "I'm Don Cornelius, and as always in parting, we wish you love, peace, and soul!"

DOO-WOP: A genre of music developed in the 1940s by Black people in large cities such as Los Angeles and New York, doo-wop usually features a four-part group harmony with minimal instrumentation.

DORIS MILLER (1919–1943): A Black American Navy soldier who, for his actions at Pearl Harbor, became the first Black American to receive the Navy Cross. Miller was killed in action in 1943.

DOROTHY DANDRIDGE (1922–1965): A Black American actor, dancer, and singer who found early success during the 1940s and 1950s and starred in films including *Carmen Jones* (1954), *Island in the Sun* (1957) and *Porgy and Bess* (1959).

DOUGLAS WILDER (1931–): a Black American politician and lawyer who served as the 66th governor of Virginia. When he was elected in 1990, he became the first Black American to serve as governor since Reconstruction.

DUKE ELLINGTON (1899–1974): A Black American composer and musician who began his career in 1923 at the dawn of the Harlem Renaissance. His career spanned over five decades; his most recognized works include "It Don't Mean a Thing" (1943), "Mood Indigo" (1930), and "Take the 'A' Train" (1939).

DUST BOWL: Refers to the period of severe drought in North America that lasted from 1930 to 1936 as well as to the area of land where the vegetation was lost due to soil erosion and unsustainable farming practices. Contrary to historical narratives, the Dust Bowl adversely impacted indigenous people and Black people in addition to its more commonly discussed impact on white farmers.

EBONY: Founded in Chicago by John H. Johnson, *Ebony* magazine is a source of Black news, politics, and culture for Black communities, dating back to 1945.

ED SMALLS (1882–1974): A Black American entrepreneur and proprietor of Smalls Paradise, a Harlem nightclub that, unlike similar clubs of the era, was racially integrated. Smalls founded the club in 1925 and sold the establishment in 1959.

EDUCATION FOR ALL HANDICAPPED CHILDREN ACT (1975): Legislation enacted by the U.S. Congress in 1975 following pressure from disability rights activists. The act required all American public schools accepting federal funds to provide free specialized education services to children with disabilities.

EDWIN STARR (1942–2003): A Black American singer-songwriter who created music using the influences of soul, blues, funk, and disco. He became famous following his 1970s hit song "War," which captured the energy of antiwar protesters speaking up against the Vietnam War.

EIGHTEENTH AMENDMENT (1920): The first and only amendment to be repealed from the U.S. Constitution. The Eighteenth Amendment banned the sale and consumption of alcohol in the United States and was in effect from 1920 to 1933.

EL HAJJ MALIK EL SHABAZZ (1925–1965): Known also as Malcolm X, Shabazz was a Black American Muslim Pan-Africanist civil rights leader. In the early 1950s, he joined the Nation of Islam and used media to spread the message of its leader, Elijah Muhammad. In the 1960s, he cut ties with the Nation of Islam and converted to Sunni Islam. Prior to his assassination, Shabazz formed the short-lived Sunni organization Muslim Mosque, Inc., and the Pan-Africanist group the Organization of Afro-American Unity.

ELEANOR ROOSEVELT (1884–1962): A white American political figure, diplomat, and activist. She served as the First Lady of the United States from March 4, 1933, to April 12, 1945, during her husband President Franklin D. Roosevelt's four terms in office, making her the longest-serving First Lady.

ELIJAH MUHAMMAD (1897–1975): A Black American religious leader who led the Nation of Islam from 1934 until his death in 1975.

ELLA BAKER (1903–1986): A Black American civil rights and human rights activist. Her work in activism spanned over five decades and included the cofounding of the Southern Christian Leadership Conference (SCLC) and the Student Nonviolent Coordinating Committee (SNCC).

ELLA FITZGERALD (1917–1996): A Black American jazz singer. Known also as the First Lady of Song, Queen of Jazz, and Lady Ella, Fitzgerald was world renowned for her improvisational scat singing, as well as her ability to convey profound messages through her vocalizations.

ELLIS ISLAND: A former U.S. immigration processing station, located in the New York Harbor on the state borders of New York and New Jersey. Between 1892 and 1954, Ellis Island processed over twelve million immigrants to the United States. Today, Ellis Island is a museum.

ELVIS PRESLEY (1935–1977): A white American singer and actor who popularized the musical genre of rock 'n' roll. Some of his most recognized songs include "Blue Suede Shoes" (1956), "Jailhouse Rock" (1957), and "Hound Dog" (1957), which was originally sung by Black American singer Big Mama Thornton in 1953.

EMANCIPATION PROCLAMATION (1863): An order issued by President Abraham Lincoln during the Civil War to incite political and military instability within the Confederate States by ordering the freeing of enslaved people. While it marked the beginning of the end for chattel slavery, it applied only to the Confederate States, meaning that states that participated in slavery but did not leave the Union were not obligated to free enslaved people.

EMMA GOLDMAN (1869–1940): A Russian political activist of Jewish faith who promoted the notion of absolute freedom in all facets of life. In 1916, she was arrested in New York City for lecturing and distributing materials about birth control, and although she spent fifteen days in prison, she continued to advocate for reproductive freedom, sexual freedom, religious freedom, and more, until her passing.

EMMETT TILL (1941–1955): A fourteen-year-old Black American who was lynched in Mississippi in 1955, following fallacious accusations made by a white woman. Till attended

McCosh Elementary School in Chicago and was laid to rest in Burr Oak Cemetery in a suburb of Chicago on September 6, 1995. Till's brutal murder became the catalyst for further migration out of the rural South and for increased action during the Civil Rights movement to protect Black youth.

EXECUTIVE ORDER: In the United States, the president, through the use of an executive order, has the power to issue rules to the military or other parts of the executive branch of the government that must be obeyed as law.

FANNIE LOU HAMER (1917–1977): A Black American civil rights activist, community advocate, and voting rights organizer from Montgomery County, Mississippi, Hamer was also a key organizer of the 1964 Mississippi Freedom Summer and worked alongside the Student Nonviolent Coordinating Committee (SNCC).

FASCISM: A political idea that uses dictatorial power, suppressing any opposing parties often through violence and propaganda, and maintains control over social behavior, the economy, and the press.

FEDERAL BUREAU OF INVESTIGATION (FBI): An American intelligence organization working domestically for the interests of the U.S. government and not necessarily of its people. The FBI is the primary federal law enforcement agency in the United States. Historically, the FBI has been harmful to marginalized groups, including indigenous and Black people, people of color, immigrant communities, LGBTQ communities, and members of dissenting political organizations like Communists, Black Panther Party members, and more.

FEMINISM: The advocacy of women's rights and the rights of historically marginalized genders for the political, economic, and social equality of and between the many genders. In the United States specifically, feminism has a long and complex history for indigenous people, Black people, and people of color because feminist advocacy has often excluded people who do not conform to traditional expressions of womanhood and femininity.

FEMINIST: A person who, regardless of gender, supports feminism.

FIFTEENTH AMENDMENT (1869): This amendment prohibited federal and state governments from denying U.S. citizens the right to vote based on race, color, or past servitude, thus extending voting rights to Black men.

FIRST GREAT MIGRATION: The period of the first Great Migration began in the 1910s during World War I and concluded with the Great Depression during the 1930s. During this period, about 1.6 million people moved from rural areas in the South to northern and western cities like Detroit, where industrial jobs drew communities from the South.

FIRST-WAVE FEMINISM: A period of feminist activity that took place between the late nineteenth and early twentieth centuries, first-wave feminism focused on legal issues, primarily on gaining the right to vote.

FOURTEENTH AMENDMENT (1868): This amendment defined an American citizen as any person born in or "naturalized" in the United States. It also overturned the U.S. Supreme Court's decision in the *Dred Scott* case (1857), which had ruled that Black people were not eligible for citizenship.

FRANKLIN DELANO ROOSEVELT (1882–1945): Also known as FDR, Roosevelt was a white American politician who served as the 32nd president of the United States from 1933 until his death in 1945. FDR was the longest-serving president of the United States and was married to Eleanor Roosevelt. FDR also authorized the forced internment of Japanese Americans and people of Japanese descent in American concentration camps during World War II.

FRED HAMPTON (1948–1969): A Black American revolutionary activist who served as the Illinois chairman of the Black Panther Party. Hampton was twenty-one years old when the FBI and Chicago police collaborated to assassinate him on December 4, 1969. Before his death, Hampton negotiated a pact to end violence between rival street gangs in Chicago and created a multicultural coalition with the Young Lords and Young Patriots Organization.

FREDERICK DOUGLASS (1818–1895): Born enslaved in 1818, Douglass was a prominent Black American abolitionist leader, writer, and orator who advocated for suffrage across gender and race in addition to the abolition of slavery.

FREEDMEN'S BUREAU: The U.S. Congress established the Freedmen's Bureau under President Abraham Lincoln's administration to settle, educate, and aid the millions of freed Black people and white people who had been devastated by the aftermath of the Civil War and the dying Southern economy.

FREEDOM RIDES: A Civil Rights–era peaceful protest initiative wherein Black and white activists called Freedom Riders rode buses from station to station, using facilities along the way, between May 4, 1961, and December 10, 1961.

FREEDOM SUMMER (1964): A voter education and registration campaign organized by Fannie Lou Hamer and the Council of Federated Organizations (COFO), which consisted of the Mississippi branches of the Student Nonviolent Coordinating Committee (SNCC), the Congress of Racial Equality (CORE), the National Association for the Advancement of Colored People (NAACP), and the Southern Christian Leadership Conference (SCLC). It recruited volunteers from across the country to canvas and register Black Mississippians to vote even against threats of violence.

GARVEYISM: An ideology created by Marcus Garvey that urges the complete self-reliance of Black people globally, including military, economic, and political independence.

GENDER EQUALITY: The state of equal access by people of all genders to opportunity, decision making, moral authority, resources, and more without regard to gender.

GEORGE EDMUND HAYNES (1880–1960): A Black American scholar who in 1911 became cofounder and executive director of the National Urban League, serving from its founding until 1918. Haynes also cofounded the magazine *Opportunity: A Journal of Negro Life* in 1923.

GEORGIA BLACK (1906–1951): A Black American transgender woman from South Carolina. In 1951, *Ebony* magazine outed her on a national level and reported her story with disrespectful and sensationalist overtones. In 2012, Monica Roberts retold Black's story with the honor and dignity she deserved. Black was an active member of her church, a beloved member of the community, a mother, and a wife.

GERALD FORD (1913–2006): A white American politician who served as the 38th president of the United States. Ford was nominated by President Nixon to serve as vice president following the resignation of Spiro Agnew in 1973. When Nixon resigned in 1974, Ford became president, and one month after taking office, he pardoned Nixon, absolving the former president of all wrongdoing.

GHETTO: In the context of the United States, a ghetto is a neighborhood in a city characterized by dilapidated housing and inadequate infrastructure, which, because of institutionalized racism, is most frequently occupied by Black people and communities of color. *See also* redlining.

G.I. BILL (1944): Also known as the Servicemen's Readjustment Act (1944), the G.I. Bill afforded housing, work, and education to returning veterans but did not contain language to ensure that those benefits were equally distributed across race.

GIL SCOTT-HERON (1949–2011): A Black American soul and jazz poet, musician, and artist primarily known for using a style of spoken word poetry to advocate for social and political issues throughout the 1970s and 1980s. Scott-Heron's most popular poems include "The Revolution Will Not Be Televised" (1970) and "Home Is Where the Hatred Is" (1971).

GLADYS BENTLEY (1907–1960): A Black lesbian American entertainer who became famous during the Harlem Renaissance for her bold performances, where she was known to sing salacious lyrics and openly flirt with women in the audience.

GREAT DEPRESSION: The Great Depression was a severe worldwide economic depression that took place mostly during the 1930s, beginning in the United States with the stock market collapse in 1929. The world economy did not fully recover from this collapse until World War II.

GREAT MIGRATION: The internal migration from 1900 to 1979 of over six million Black Americans from the rural South to the urban and industrial centers of the West, Midwest, and North. *See also* **First Great Migration and Second Great Migration.**

GREAT WAR: *See* **World War** I.

GWENDOLYN BENNETT (1902–1981): A Black American artist, writer, and journalist who contributed to *Opportunity: A Journal of Negro Life*, which chronicled cultural advancements during the Harlem Renaissance.

HARLEM HELLFIGHTERS: The first Black and Puerto Rican soldiers to see combat during World War I and the first Allied unit to cross the Rhine River in Germany during World War I. In total, these soldiers served for 191 days, the longest duration of service of any American unit during World War I, and they suffered the greatest sacrifice, with 1,500 lives lost as casualties of war. For their efforts, the French military awarded more than 170 medals to individual soldiers and awarded the high honor of the Croix de Guerre to the entire Harlem Hellfighters unit. Despite their dedication and sacrifice to their home country, they returned to face racism and segregation from their fellow countrymen.

HARLEM RENAISSANCE: Also known as the New Negro movement; named for Alain Locke's 1925 text *The New Negro*, the Harlem Renaissance was the blossoming of Black scholars, artists, writers, and musicians during the 1920s and 1930s.

HARRY BELAFONTE (1927–): A Black American singer, actor, and activist of Jamaican and Martiniquan descent, Belafonte is known for his successful film and music career and for his early and continued support of the Civil Rights movements of the past and present. Belafonte starred in films including *Bright Road* (1953), *Carmen Jones* (1954), *Island in the Sun* (1957), and *White Man's Burden* (1995). Some of Belafonte's songs include "Day-O" (1956) and "Jump in the Line" (1961).

HATTIE MCDANIEL (1895–1952): A Black American actor and singer from Wichita, Kansas. In addition to being the first Black woman to sing on the radio in the United States, she was also known for being the first Black actor to win the Academy Award for Best Supporting Actress for her role as Mammy in *Gone with the Wind* (1939).

HENDERSON V. UNITED STATES (1950): A legal case heard by the U.S. Supreme Court in 1950 that abolished segregation in railroad dining cars.

HERBERT HOOVER (1874–1964): A white American businessperson and politician who served as the 31st president of the United States from 1929 to 1933 during the early years of the Great Depression.

HIP-HOP: An influential American musical genre that emerged during the 1970s in large part because of the Great Migration. Created by young people in the Black and Latinx communities, hip-hop includes four elements: movement and break dancing, or "b-boying"; music, or "djing"; street art and style, or graffiti; and rapping, or "mc'ing."

HIRAM RHODES REVELS (1827–1901): A Black American Union Army chaplain during the Civil War, Revels, who was also a politician, became the first Black member of the U.S. Congress in 1870, serving Mississippi until 1871.

HISTORICALLY BLACK COLLEGES OR UNIVERSITIES (HBCU): Institutions that were focused on the education of Black Americans and founded prior to the Civil Rights Act of 1964 have been designated HBCUs by the U.S. Congress. By the 1930s, 121 HBCUs welcomed students of all races into their halls—years prior to the groundbreaking *Brown v. Board of Education* case that set the ball in motion for school desegregation. In 2017, 101 HBCUs remained open.

HOMOPHOBIA: The fear, hatred, disbelief, or mistrust of people who are LGBTQ, thought to be LGBTQ, or whose sexual orientation does not conform to heteronormativity or the idea that heterosexuality is the default sexual orientation.

HOMOSEXUAL: An archaic term used to describe people who are attracted to members of the same gender. Today it is an offensive term to many due to its history of use by homophobic individuals and groups to suggest that same-gender attraction is indicative of mental illness. These suggestions were espoused by the American Psychological Association until the 1970s.

HUEY P. NEWTON (1942–1989): A Black American political activist who cofounded the Black Panther Party for Self-Defense in 1966 with Bobby Seale. Newton worked alongside Seale to create the Black Panther Party's Ten-Point Platform as the strategic map for the organization and for the Black community.

IDA B. WELLS (1862–1931): Born enslaved in 1862 in Holly Springs, Mississippi, Wells was a prominent investigative journalist and civil rights leader who cataloged and investigated lynchings in the South, creating the foundational research on the subject. Wells published a book called *The Red Record* in 1895 that chronicled several lynchings as well as various indignities suffered by Black people. In 1909, Wells became one of the founders of the National Association for the Advancement of Colored People (NAACP).

IMMIGRATION ACT OF 1924: Also known as the Johnson-Reed Act, or the Asian Exclusion Act, this was a federal law inspired by prejudice. The law prevented immigrants from Asia and Eastern Europe, including Greeks, Italians, Poles, and Slavs, from entering the United States by enforcing national quotas. Jewish people were also prevented from immigrating to the United States under this law.

INDIANS OF ALL TRIBES: A Native American and indigenous civil rights group. Their members organized the occupation of Alcatraz Island from November 1969 to June 1971. *See also* **Occupation of Alcatraz Island.**

INDIGENOUS RIGHTS MOVEMENT: *See* **Red Power.**

INTERSECTIONALITY: Legal scholar Kimberlé Crenshaw developed the theory of intersectionality in order to understand the various forms of oppression in society and the ways they impact the overlapping identities of Blackness and womanhood.

J. EDGAR HOOVER (1895–1972): A white American man who, in 1924, became the first director of the Federal Bureau of Investigation (FBI) of the United States, serving a life term until 1972. As director of the FBI, Hoover abused his authority to intimidate and harass political opponents, namely Communists, civil rights and Black Power leaders, and LGBTQ people. Under Hoover, the FBI routinely surveilled community leaders and collected files on figures like El Hajj Malik El Shabazz, Dr. Martin Luther King Jr., John Lewis, and Rosa Parks. Hoover created the Counterintelligence Program (COINTELPRO) that was charged with collecting information (often through illegal means) on civil rights leaders and organizations with the goal of destabilizing the Civil Rights and Black Power movements.

JAMES BALDWIN (1924–1987): A Black queer American writer, advocate, and social critic known for contributions to the LGBTQ Rights movement and Civil Rights movement. His work included *Giovanni's Room* (1956), *The Fire Next Time* (1963), *No Name in the Street* (1972), and many more. Baldwin served on the board of the Congress of Racial Equality (CORE) and won many awards in recognition of his literary achievements.

JAMES BROWN (1933–2006): Known as the Godfather of Soul, Brown was a Black American singer, songwriter, dancer, musician, producer, and bandleader who was famous for his signature improvisational style, blending funk, jazz, and blues. He created hit songs, including "Say It Loud—I'm Black and I'm Proud" (1968), "Papa's Got a Brand New Bag" (1966), and "Get on the Good Foot" (1972).

JAMES FARMER (1920–1999): A Black American civil rights activist, Farmer cofounded the Congress of Racial Equality (CORE) in 1942 with George Houser and Bernice Fisher. During the 1960s, he was known as a major civil rights leader for his leadership in CORE.

JAMES MEREDITH (1933–): A Black American civil rights activist, writer, political adviser, and U.S. Air Force veteran. In 1962, he became the first Black American student admitted to the segregated University of Mississippi. In 1966, Meredith planned a solo March Against Fear from Memphis, Tennessee,

to Jackson, Mississippi, and continued his career in activism as a voter education and registration activist.

JESSE OWENS (1913–1980): A Black American athlete, Owens was born in 1913 in Oakville, Alabama, to sharecropper parents. In 1935, he qualified for the 1936 Berlin Summer Olympics and won four Olympic gold medals.

JIM CROW: The term "Jim Crow" comes from a caricature of Black men that was popularized by white minstrel singers who performed racist stereotypes of Black people while wearing blackface. "Jim Crow" also refers to the policies and laws that enforced racial segregation throughout the southern United States following the end of chattel slavery. Jim Crow laws segregated schools, drinking fountains, bathrooms, and other facilities with infamous "Whites Only" and "Coloreds Only" signs, rampant police violence, and domestic terrorism.

JIVE: A term that may refer to many elements of Black American culture, including dance and music, but is most often used in reference to African American English used in the latter half of the Great Migration between the 1940s and 1970s.

JOE LOUIS (1911–1981): A Black American boxer from Alabama, Louis began his boxing career in 1934 and went on to win the heavyweight title in 1937 after defeating a white boxer named James Braddock; he held that title until 1949. Today, Louis is considered to have been one of the greatest heavyweight boxers in U.S. sporting history.

JOHN CARLOS (1945–): A Black American track and field athlete, Carlos was born in 1945 in Harlem, New York, and was the son of Afro–Cuban parents. Carlos used his platform as an Olympian to advocate for human rights, most notably during the 1968 Mexico City Summer Olympics, when he and Tommie Smith took the podium with a reverent lowered gaze and hands raised defiantly in the

Black Power salute, as the national anthem sounded in the background.

JOHN F. KENNEDY (1917–1963): America's 35th president, Kennedy was a white politician who was elected in 1960 and served until his assasination in 1963. He was the first Catholic U.S. president.

JOHN LEWIS (1940–): In 1961, Lewis, a Black American activist, volunteered to participate in the Freedom Rides, which challenged segregation at interstate bus terminals across the southern United States. From 1963 to 1966, Lewis was chairman of the Student Nonviolent Coordinating Committee (SNCC). At the age of twenty-three, he was an architect of and a keynote speaker at the historic 1963 March on Washington for Jobs and Freedom. Lewis has served as U.S. representative of Georgia's 5th Congressional District since 1987. He is the coauthor of the graphic novel trilogy *MARCH*, which is about the Freedom Rides and the SNCC.

JOHN STEINBECK (1902–1968): A white American author whose books *Of Mice and Men* (1937) and *The Grapes of Wrath* (1939) are considered to be primers on the hardships faced by Americans during the 1930s, even though his texts present glaring omissions of the Black community and other communities of color.

JUNETEENTH: Taking place annually on June 19, Juneteenth, or Emancipation Day, is the official day that chattel enslavement ended in the United States. On this day in 1865, Texas finally adhered to the order of emancipation and freed its remaining enslaved people.

KEN BURNS (1953–): A white American filmmaker who is known for using archival footage and photographs in documentary films. While his documentaries *Jazz* (2001) and *The Vietnam War* (2017) include robust discussions of the realities faced by Black people and other people of color, his documentaries *The Dust Bowl* (2012), *The Civil War* (1990),

The War (2007), *The National Parks: America's Best Idea* (2009), and *Prohibition* (2011) center on white people and white men in particular.

KENNETH CLARK (1914–2005): A Black American social psychologist who developed foundational research on Black self-identity in children. Alongside his wife, Dr. Mamie Clark, Dr. Clark identified the ways that Jim Crow laws adversely impacted the self-identify of Black children. His most significant study, the Doll Test, was used in the *Brown v. Board of Education* (1954) case. The study found that Black children were internalizing feelings of inferiority because of racial segregation.

KING TUTANKHAMEN (1341–1323 BCE): King Tut, as he is also known, was an Egyptian pharaoh of the 18th dynasty during the period of Egyptian history known as the New Kingdom or sometimes the New Empire Period. In 1923, his tomb was discovered and inspired a renewed interest in African history.

KOREAN WAR (1950–1953): Also known as the Forgotten War, the Korean War began on June 25, 1950, and ended on July 27, 1953, with the signing of the Korean Armistice Agreement, which allowed for the return of prisoners. But no peace treaty has yet been signed, so technically, the two Koreas are still in frozen conflict with the boundary between them set at the 38th parallel. The war was mostly fought between North Korea, with the support of China and the Soviet Union, and South Korea, which had the support of the UK and the United States. Including both military and civilian populations, an estimated 2.5 million people died as a result of this war.

KU KLUX KLAN (KKK): A white supremacist hate group founded in 1865 and based in the United States, the KKK has been responsible for acts of domestic terror against Black people, Jewish people, LGBTQ people, and communities of color since the Reconstruction era.

KWAME TURE (1941–1998): Known also as Stokely Carmichael, Ture was a Trinidadian American organizer and leader within the Civil Rights and Black Power movements. Ture began his activism while attending Howard University and continued his work until his death. Ture served as chairman of the Student Nonviolent Coordinating Committee (SNCC); an honorary member of the Black Panther Party; and a leader of the Pan-Africanist organization, the All-African People's Revolutionary Party.

KWANZAA: Created by Ron Karenga in 1966, Kwanzaa is a Pan-Africanist holiday honoring Black people and focuses on seven key values that Karenga believed were central to African heritage. Taking place over seven days, each day is dedicated to a different value, each one translated from Swahili. These include *Umoja*, or unity; *Kujichagulia*, or self-determination; *Ujima*, or collective work and responsibility; *Ujamaa*, or cooperative economics; *Nia*, or purpose; *Kuumba*, or creativity; and *Imani*, or faith. Black people globally celebrate Kwanzaa annually from December 26 to January 1.

LANGSTON HUGHES (1902–1967): A prolific Black American author, activist, and poet, Hughes rose to prominence during the Harlem Renaissance in the 1920s. His work explores Black American identity and ideology. Notable poems and essays by Hughes include "Let America Be America Again" (1935), "The Negro Artist and the Racial Mountain" (1926), "I, Too" (1926), and "Harlem" (1951).

LARRY ITLIONG (1913–1977): A Filipino American labor rights organizer, Itliong organized and participated in the 1965 Delano grape strike, co-led by the Agricultural Workers Organizing Committee and the United Farm Workers against grape growers in California. Over a period of five years, the strike resulted in a mutually agreed upon contract that provided workers with better working conditions and a minimum wage.

LATINX: A gender-neutral umbrella term, Latinx describes people from many countries, cultures, and races who are united by a shared history as descendants of the colonization of North, Central, and South America. Latinx is often used in place of the gendered designations of Latina and Latino.

LEGAL DEFENSE FUND: *See* NAACP.

LENA HORNE (1917–2010): A Black American singer, dancer, actor, and civil rights activist. Her career spanned over seventy years, and she appeared in film, television, and theater. Some of Horne's most famous films include *Stormy Weather* (1943) and *The Wiz* (1978).

LEVAR BURTON (1957–): An American actor, educator, and activist, Burton became a household name in 1977 with his portrayal of the young Kunta Kinte, the main character in the television miniseries *Roots*. During his career, which spans decades, Burton has also portrayed Geordi La Forge in *Star Trek* and himself in *Reading Rainbow*, a series that taught millions of children how to be enthusiastic and confident readers using television.

LGBTQ: This acronym is formed based on the following terms: lesbian, gay, bisexual, transgender, and queer. The acronym is often expanded to LGBTQIA+, which includes intersex, asexual, and other groups that fall along the spectrum of gender and sexual orientation.

LGBTQ LIBERATION: *See* LGBTQ *Rights Movement.*

LGBTQ RIGHTS MOVEMENT: An ongoing social movement for the equal acceptance of LGBTQ people in society. Following the Stonewall Riots in 1969, the LGBTQ Rights movement began using direct action mobilization to confront homophobic and transphobic legislation and policies.

LINDA BROWN (1943–2018): A Black American civil rights activist who, in 1954, became the center of the landmark U.S. civil rights case *Brown v. Board of Education* (1954), which resulted in the long-held "separate but equal" doctrine established in the *Plessy v. Ferguson* case being dismantled.

LITERACY TESTS: A series of questions aimed at disqualifying people from being able to register to vote. Literacy test laws were used to target Black people, because they had higher rates of illiteracy due to unequal educational opportunities.

LITTLE RICHARD (1932–): An openly queer Black American singer, pianist, and stage performer, Little Richard was known for his theatrical showmanship and improvisational style. His songs include "Tutti Frutti" (1957), "Good Golly, Miss Molly" (1958), and "Keep a Knockin'" (1957).

LITTLE ROCK NINE: Following the 1954 U.S. Supreme Court decision in *Brown v. Board of Education* (1954), racial segregation in schools was deemed unconstitutional. Nine students from Little Rock, Arkansas, volunteered with a local chapter of the National Association for the Advancement of Colored People (NAACP) to be the first students to integrate Little Rock Central High School. The nine students were Ernest Green, Elizabeth Eckford, Jefferson Thomas, Terrence Roberts, Carlotta Walls LaNier, Minnijean Brown, Gloria Ray Karlmark, Thelma Mothershed, and Melba Pattillo Beals. By the end of September 1957, the nine were admitted to Little Rock Central High under the protection of the 101st Airborne Division, although they were subjected to a year of physical and verbal abuse and harassment by their white peers.

LORRAINE HANSBERRY (1930–1965): A Black American LGBTQ activist and playwright. Her work reflects on the hardships of the Black community in the United States. Hansberry's most famous play was *A Raisin in the Sun* (1959), which earned her the distinction of being the first Black playwright and the youngest American to win a New York Drama Critics' Circle award. She also became the first Black woman to stage a Broadway play.

LOUIS ARMSTRONG (1901–1971): Known also as Satchmo, Armstrong was a Black American trumpeter, composer, singer, and actor who became one of the most influential figures in jazz, starting during the Harlem Renaissance.

LUCINDA TODD (1903–1996): A Black American teacher and education activist, Todd was one of the petitioners alongside thirteen other Black parents who brought the class action lawsuit that became *Brown v. Board of Education* (1954).

LYNCHING: A premeditated public execution of an individual or individuals by a group is known as a lynching. In the context of the United States, lynchings were most often committed against Black people by white supremacist hate groups with the aim of intimidating and traumatizing Black communities.

MA RAINEY (1886–1939): A Black American professional blues singer, Rainey was regarded as the Mother of the Blues and was among the first generation of blues singers to record. While she never came out during her lifetime, she did write and sing songs that referenced bisexuality and lesbian identity.

MADAM C. J. WALKER (1867–1919): A Black American entrepreneur, philanthropist, and activist who founded Madam C. J. Walker Manufacturing Company. Walker was the first self-made woman millionaire in the United States. Walker made her fortune by developing and marketing a line of cosmetics and hair care products for Black women.

MALCOLM X: *See* **El Hajj Malik El Shabazz.**

MAMIE CLARK (1917–1983): A Black American social psychologist who developed foundational research on Black self-identity in children. A study called the Doll Test, which she developed with her husband, Dr. Kenneth Clark, was used in the *Brown v. Board of Education* (1954) case. The study found that Black children were internalizing feelings of inferiority because of racial segregation. Following this landmark study, Dr. Clark continued to study Black psychology and the impacts of policy on mental health in children.

MAMIE TILL (1921–2003): A Black American educator who, following the brutal murder of her fourteen-year-old son, Emmett Till, became a civil rights activist while continuing her work as an educator, spending a total of twenty-three years teaching in the Chicago public school system.

MARCH ON WASHINGTON (1963): Also known as the March on Washington for Jobs and Freedom, this protest was organized by A. Philip Randolph and Bayard Rustin. The march consisted of a coalition of civil rights organizations under the mission of "jobs and freedom." The August 28 event drew more than two hundred thousand participants and is remembered for the speech "I Have a Dream," delivered by Dr. Martin Luther King Jr. in front of the Lincoln Memorial.

MARCUS GARVEY (1887–1940): A Jamaican-born political leader, Garvey founded the Universal Negro Improvement Association and African Communities League (UNIA–ACL) in 1914 after being inspired by his travels across the Caribbean and Central America. His ideology, Garveyism, emphasizes the complete self-reliance of Black people globally. Garveyism inspired the strategies of many movements, including the Nation of Islam, Pan-Africanism, and the Black Power movement.

MARIAN ANDERSON (1897–1993): A Black American singer who, starting during the Harlem Renaissance, performed around the world, in the United States, and in Europe between 1925 and 1965. In 1955, she became the first Black American to perform with the New York Metropolitan Opera.

MARIAN WRIGHT EDELMAN (1939–): A Black American human rights advocate who in 1973 founded the Children's Defense Fund to focus on disabled children, poor children, and children of color. She was the first African American woman admitted to the Mississippi Bar.

MARSHA P. JOHNSON (1945–1992): A transgender Black American LGBTQ rights activist, Johnson was known for her role in the LGBTQ Rights movement in the United States.

MARTIN LUTHER KING JR. (1929–1968): A Black American religious leader known for his role in advancing the Civil Rights movement through the practice of nonviolent direct action. He fought for voting rights and LGBTQ equality, and against poverty, war, militarism, racism, and materialism. King was married to Coretta Scott King and had four children, Bernice King, Dexter King, Martin Luther King III, and Yolanda King.

MARVIN GAYE (1939–1984): A Black American singer, songwriter, and producer, Gaye helped craft the style of Motown Record's early artists during the 1960s. After he pressured Motown producers to allow artists to discuss activism in their music, he released songs including "What's Going On" (1971) and "Mercy Mercy Me" (1968). Some of Gaye's love songs include "Sexual Healing" (1982) and "Ain't No Mountain High Enough" (1966).

MARY MCLEOD BETHUNE (1875–1955): A Black American education advocate and influential advisor to President Franklin D. Roosevelt, Bethune founded and became the first director of the National Youth Administration's Office of Negro Affairs during President Roosevelt's second term in office.

MASON–DIXON LINE: Also called the Mason and Dixon line, this boundary was surveyed between 1763 and 1767 by Charles Mason and Jeremiah Dixon to resolve a border dispute involving Maryland, Pennsylvania, and Delaware in Colonial America. Later on, this line delineated the states in which slavery was legal and the states that had abolished slavery. Today, the line is used to define the border between the American South and North.

MCLAURIN V. OKLAHOMA STATE REGENTS (1950): This U.S. Supreme Court case involved George W. McLaurin and the Oklahoma State Regents for Higher Education. McLaurin was pursuing a PhD and had been denied entry to the University of Oklahoma's doctorate program because Oklahoma law prohibited schools from integrating. In 1950, the U.S. Supreme Court held that the different treatment of students in public institutions of higher learning solely on the basis of race violated the Equal Protection Clause of the Fourteenth Amendment.

MEDGAR EVERS (1925–1963): A Black American civil rights leader from Mississippi, Evers was a veteran of World War II and was the Mississippi field secretary for the National Association for the Advancement of Colored People (NAACP). He organized many civil rights actions and worked toward the achievement of civil rights until his assassination by a white supremacist in 1963.

THE MESSENGER: A. Philip Randolph and Chandler Owen founded this magazine, which was published from 1917 until 1928, in New York City during the Harlem Renaissance. The magazine provided a platform to many emerging writers during the Harlem Renaissance and strengthened Black culture, ideology, and identity during the early twentieth century. The publication was also investigated by the U.S. government after publishing dissenting political essays on Garveyism and Pan-Africanism.

MONTGOMERY BUS BOYCOTT (1955): A protest campaign against the policy of racial segregation on the public transit system of Montgomery, Alabama, that lasted from 1955 to 1956. While the boycott started after the arrest of the National Association for the Advancement of Colored People (NAACP)'s regional secretary, Rosa Parks, it would not have been successful without the contributions of the entire Montgomery, Alabama, community as well as the sacrifices of Claudette Colvin, Aurelia Browder, Susie McDonald, and Mary Louise Smith, who had been arrested for refusing to give up their seats to white passengers months before the actions Parks undertook.

MOORISH SCIENCE TEMPLE OF AMERICA: This religious organization, which was founded by Noble Drew Ali in 1913 in the United States, teaches that Black Americans are the descendants of the Moorish people and should follow Islamic teachings.

MOTOWN RECORDS: A music label founded by Berry Gordy in 1959 as Tamla Records, and renamed Motown records in 1960. Classic Motown artists include Diana Ross, Stevie Wonder, and Marvin Gaye, all of whom are credited with defining American music.

MUHAMMAD ALI (1942–2016): A Black American Muslim, Ali was a professional boxer and antiwar activist from Louisville, Kentucky. In 1954, he began his boxing career, and in 1964, he defeated Sonny Liston and won the world heavyweight championship. Ali was often called The Greatest, and his legacy of activism and athletic prowess led many to regard him as one of the greatest athletes of all time.

MYRLIE EVERS-WILLIAMS (1933–): A Black American civil rights activist and author. Following the assassination of her late husband, Medgar Evers, she worked tirelessly to solidify his legacy and to pursue investigations into his murder. She also served as chairwoman of the National Association for the Advancement of Colored People (NAACP) and is the author of *For Us, The Living* (1967) and *Watch Me Fly: What I Learned on the Way to Becoming the Woman I Was Meant to Be* (1999).

NAT KING COLE (1919–1965): A Black American jazz pianist and vocalist. In 1956, he became the first Black American performer to host a television variety series called *The Nat King Cole Show*.

NATION OF ISLAM: A religious order of Black American Muslims, the Nation of Islam was founded in 1930 by Master W. Fard Muhammad. Members of the Nation of Islam believe that the Islamic figure Prophet Muhammad was the last prophet of Allah, and that Elijah Muhammad was his messenger, taught by God in the person of the Mahdi, or Master W. Fard Muhammad.

NATIONAL ASSOCIATION FOR THE ADVANCEMENT OF COLORED PEOPLE (NAACP): Founded on February 12, 1909, to establish legal protections, educational opportunities, and social support for Black people across the country, the NAACP is the nation's oldest, largest, and most widely recognized grassroots-based civil rights organization.

NATIONAL NEGRO BUSINESS LEAGUE (NNBL): Booker T. Washington founded the NNBL in Boston in 1900 "to promote the commercial and financial development" of the Black community. Today it continues operation as the National Business League.

NATIONAL URBAN LEAGUE: In 1911, Dr. George Edmund Haynes and Ruth Standish Baldwin founded the National Urban League to provide social support and education to the growing number of Black people in urban areas like New York and St. Louis.

THE NEGRO MOTORIST GREEN BOOK: Victor Hugo Green published this annual guidebook from 1936 to 1966. Based on similar materials created by and for Jewish travelers, *The Negro Motorist Green Book* provided a list of accommodations, gas stations, restaurants, and hotels that accepted Black travelers.

NEW DEAL: Between 1933 and 1936, President Franklin D. Roosevelt enacted the New Deal, which was a series of programs, public works projects, financial reforms, and regulations. The New Deal responded to the need for relief, reform, and recovery from the Great Depression.

NEW NEGRO MOVEMENT: *See* **Harlem Renaissance**.

OCCUPATION OF ALCATRAZ ISLAND: Led by the Indians of All Tribes organization, the Occupation of Alcatraz Island lasted from November 20, 1969, to June 11, 1971, a nineteen-month period. During this time, Native American organizers took over Alcatraz Island, a small island in San Francisco Bay, and reoccupied it as Native American territory. At its height, the occupation included eighty-nine organizers and lifted the struggles of Native Americans to an international level.

OLIVER BROWN (1918–1961): Born in Springfield, Missouri, Brown served as a welder for rail companies during his adulthood. In 1950, he was recruited to be part of a lawsuit against the Topeka, Kansas, Board of Education in a National Association for the Advancement of Colored People (NAACP) legal action with thirteen other families that resulted in the *Brown v. Board of Education* case.

ONE CENT SAVINGS BANK: Founded in 1904 in Nashville, Tennessee, by Richard H. Boyd, the One Cent Savings Bank is known today as Citizens Bank and is the oldest continuously operating African American–owned bank in the country.

OPPORTUNITY: A JOURNAL OF NEGRO LIFE: This journal was published by the National Urban League from 1923 to 1949.

OSCAR DE PRIEST (1871–1951): A Black American politician born in Alabama and raised in Chicago who, from 1929 to 1935, served as the U.S. representative from Illinois's 1st Congressional District. De Priest advocated for anti-discrimination language to appear in the legislation that comprised the New Deal programs.

P. B. S. PINCHBACK (1837–1921): A Black American politician from Macon, Georgia, Pinckney Benton Stewart Pinchback, or P. B. S. Pinchback, served as governor of Louisiana after the former governor was suspended from office.

PATOIS: Patois includes a variety of dialects that are often a combination of one or more languages generally spoken by Francophone people of African descent in the Caribbean, North America, and South America; it may also refer to Jamaican patois.

PATRIARCHY: A form of social structure that prioritizes men in positions of leadership, moral authority, and economic control.

PAULI MURRAY (1910–1985): A Black queer American activist, civil rights leader, lawyer, and ordained deacon and priest who studied and published works on feminism, intersectionality (before the term was coined), and gender theory. Murray's works include *Proud Shoes* (1956) and *Dark Testament and Other Poems* (1970).

PEARL HARBOR (1941): Pearl Harbor is a U.S. naval base near Honolulu, Hawaii, that on December 7, 1941, was the scene of a devastating surprise attack by the Imperial Japanese Navy Air Service forces. The attack claimed the lives of 2,403 American servicemen and civilians and became the catalyst for American involvement in World War II.

PIERRE CALISTE LANDRY (1841–1921): Born enslaved in 1841, Landry was sold away from his family at the age of thirteen for under $2,000 (approximately $60,000 when adjusted for today's inflation). Likely due to his privilege as a light-skinned, mixed-race Black person, Landry was able to pursue an education during his adolescence and into adulthood, despite being enslaved. When the Thirteenth Amendment freed enslaved people, Landry opened schools for Black children who were now free to attain literacy as well as a general education. He became a prominent member of the community in Donaldsonville, Louisiana, where he was elected mayor in 1868, becoming the first Black mayor of a U.S. city. Landry went on to found the third Historically Black College or University (HBCU) in Louisiana, which was renamed Dillard University in 1935.

PLESSY V. FERGUSON (1896): The U.S. Supreme Court in 1896 heard the *Plessy v. Ferguson* case, which concerned racial discrimination and segregation on public transportation. The decision reached by the court held that as long as the segregated facilities were "equal," segregation was constitutional. This decision came to be known as the "separate but equal" doctrine, which became the justification for Jim Crow laws across the United States, until the U.S. Supreme Court overturned this decision during the landmark cases of the Civil Rights movement.

POLL TAXES: Voting fees imposed on otherwise eligible voters, poll taxes were required to be paid before a voter could cast a ballot. Poll taxes excluded most people of color and poor people, because they were economically disadvantaged and could not afford to pay the tax.

PREJUDICE: Attitudes of hostility directed against a given individual or group made prior to actual knowledge of or experience with the individuals or groups.

PRIDE: The annual celebrations of the LGBTQ community usually take place in June to honor the June 1969 Stonewall Riots, which took place in New York City.

PULLMAN PORTERS: Black men hired to work as personal attendants in the sleeping quarters of luxury railcars. Like enslaved people during the institution of slavery, Pullman porters were expected to respond to the name George after George Pullman, the owner of the Pullman Company.

RACE RIOTS: This archaic term describes violence against communities of color, most often Black communities, perpetrated by white people and European immigrants.

RACISM: The prejudiced treatment, stereotyping, or discrimination of people of color on the basis of race is called racism. Racism also refers to the system of social advantage and disadvantage or privilege and oppression that is based on race.

RACIST: A person who belongs to a dominant or privileged group that discriminates against people of other races or someone who believes that a particular race is superior to another.

RAY CHARLES (1930–2004): A blind Black American artist, singer, and musician, Charles contributed to blues, gospel, and soul music throughout his career, which spanned from 1947 until his death in 2004. Some of Charles's most popular songs include "Mess Around" (1957), "Hit the Road, Jack" (1961), and "I Got a Woman" (1957).

RECONSTRUCTION: Refers to both the period of time between 1865 and 1877 and the laws and policies created after the end of the Civil War. This period aimed to rebuild the South politically and economically while providing aid to formerly enslaved Black people, and it continued until Rutherford B. Hayes was elected president and dismantled the infrastructure that had been created.

RED POWER: Also known as the Indigenous Rights movement, the Red Power movement focused on the establishment of cultural, political, and social institutions created by and for the Native American community.

REDLINING: A discriminatory practice once encouraged by the Federal Housing Administration, redlining systematically denies loans to Black families, families of color, and poor families. The term redlining comes from the government practice of creating maps where neighborhoods outlined in red were bad and those outlined in green were good; these areas also correlated to where Black and white communities, respectively, had settled.

REPARATIONS: In the context of the United States, reparations describe payments and programs aimed at compensating the descendants of enslaved people, namely the descendants of enslaved African peoples, who were forced to work for generations under the system of chattel slavery. To this day, no such program has ever been instituted.

RESPECTABILITY: Refers to a practice of policing within marginalized groups where leaders urge community adherence to the social values of the dominant group, such as "proper" dress, conduct, and speech, with the goal of winning the favor of the dominant group.

RICHARD B. NUGENT (1906–1987): An openly gay Black American poet and artist, Nugent gained prominence during the Harlem Renaissance. He is the author of the poem "Shadow" (1925) and the short story "Smoke, Lilies and Jade" (1926).

RICHARD H. BOYD (1843–1922): Born into slavery, Boyd founded the National Baptist Publishing Board and cofounded the National Baptist Convention of America. As early as the 1890s, Boyd warned that the U.S. government would undo progress made by the Black community following the Civil War and created institutions to protect against it.

RICHARD OAKES (1942–1972): A Native American activist and Mohawk tribal member. Oakes's work resulted in the proliferation of Native American studies in university curricula. He is credited with helping to change the U.S. government termination policies of Native American peoples and culture.

RICHARD WRIGHT (1908–1960): A Black American author and poet who gained prominence during the Harlem Renaissance. Wright's work explored the violence faced by Black people in the United States. He is the author of *Uncle Tom's Children* (1938), *Native Son* (1940), and *Black Boy* (1945).

ROBERT F. KENNEDY (1925–1968): A white American lawyer and politician, Kennedy served as the 64th U.S. attorney general from 1961 to 1964 and as a U.S. senator serving New York from 1965 until his assassination in June 1968.

ROCK 'N' ROLL: Black blues, gospel, jazz, and country musicians established this popular American music genre during the 1940s and 1950s.

RON KARENGA (1941–): A Black American professor of African American history, Karenga created Kwanzaa in 1966 as a Pan-Africanist holiday. While he claimed to represent Pan-Africanism, his abuse and violence toward Black women revealed his investment in oppressing Black people.

ROOTS: Based on Alex Haley's 1976 novel of the same name, this 1977 eight-part television miniseries tells the story of Haley's descendants, starting with Kunta Kinte, who was portrayed by LeVar Burton, and continues down to Haley himself.

ROSA PARKS (1913–2005): A Black American civil rights organizer best known for her role in the 1955 Montgomery bus boycotts. Parks is the author of the memoirs *Rosa Parks: My Story* (1992) and *Quiet Strength* (1995).

ROSIE THE RIVETER: A propaganda character created in 1942 by artist J. Howard Miller to inspire women—and white women in particular—to join the workforce during World War II.

RUTH STANDISH BALDWIN (1865–1934): A white American philanthropist who used her family's wealth and the wealth of her husband, a railroad tycoon, to fund community service initiatives. In 1911, she became cofounder of the National Urban League and continued supporting the Black community until her passing in 1934.

RUTHERFORD B. HAYES (1822–1893): A white American politician who ended the Reconstruction era during his term as America's 19th president.

SECOND GREAT MIGRATION: During this period, which started during the industrialization of World War II and ended in the late 1970s, five million Black people moved from rural areas to urban areas in major U.S. cities.

SECOND-CLASS CITIZEN: A person subjected to systematic discrimination such as disenfranchisement and segregation, despite having legal citizenship within a given country or state.

SECOND-WAVE FEMINISM: During this period of feminist activity that took place between the 1960s and 1980s, the focus was on feminist scholarship and the implementation of feminist policy.

SELECTIVE SERVICE ACT (1917): Also called the Selective Draft Act, this act was enacted during World War I on May 18, 1917, and required all American men between the ages of twenty-one and thirty to register for military enlistment by national lottery. The act was canceled at the end of World War I, but American men between the ages of eighteen and twenty-five are still required to register with the Selective Service, or they cannot be eligible for federal student aid, federal job training, or a federal job.

"SEPARATE BUT EQUAL" DOCTRINE: *See Plessy v. Ferguson*.

SERVICEMEN'S READJUSTMENT ACT: *See* G.I. Bill.

SHARECROPPING: Also called tenant farming, sharecropping is a system of farming in which families pay rent to landowners in return for a portion of their crop that is to be given to the landowner at the end of each year.

SHIRLEY CHISHOLM (1924–2005): A Black American politician, educator, and author of Barbadian and Guyanese descent, Chisholm became the first Black woman elected to the U.S. Congress in 1968. She represented New York's 12th Congressional District for seven terms from 1969 to 1983. In 1972, she became the first Black woman to campaign for the Democratic Party presidential nomination with the slogan "Unbought and Unbossed."

SIDNEY POITIER (1927–): A Black American actor, director, and author of Bahamian descent. In 1964, he became the first Black actor to win an Academy Award for Best Actor and the Golden Globe Award for Best Actor for his role in *Lilies of the Field*. Poitier's most popular films include *To Sir, with Love* (1967), *The Defiant Ones* (1958), and *Porgy and Bess* (1959).

SISTER ROSETTA THARPE (1915–1973): During the late Harlem Renaissance, Tharpe, a Black American singer and songwriter, gained popularity for her gospel recordings, which blended religious themes with popular secular music. Her music became a precursor to rock 'n' roll.

SLUR: A derogatory and insulting term applied to a particular group of people, a slur is often based on harmful stereotypes.

SNYDER ACT: Known also as the Indian Citizenship Act of 1924, the Snyder Act of 1924 was named for the man who proposed it, Representative Homer P. Snyder of New York. The Snyder Act granted Native Americans full U.S. citizenship. While the Fourteenth Amendment (1868) defined citizens as any persons born or naturalized in the United States, the amendment was not interpreted to apply to Native people.

SOUTHERN TENANT FARMERS UNION (STFU): The STFU was founded in 1934 as a civil farmer's union to organize tenant farmers in the southern United States. Originally set up during the Great Depression, the STFU was founded to help sharecroppers and tenant farmers get better arrangements from landowners.

STEVIE WONDER (1950–): A blind Black American musician, songwriter, and producer known for hit songs such as "You Are the Sunshine of My Life" (1973), "Superstition" (1972), "Living for the City" (1973), "I Just Called to Say I Love You" (1984), and many more. For his decades-long career achievements, Wonder was inducted into the Rock and Roll Hall of Fame in 1989.

STONEWALL RIOTS (1969): Following an altercation between New York police and patrons of the Stonewall Inn, the Stonewall Riots took place between June 28, 1969, and July 1, 1969. Local police entered the Stonewall Inn to intimidate and harass the bar's guests, and the guests defended themselves. The night of resistance escalated into a full-scale protest, and many people were brutalized and jailed during their fight for dignity. The Stonewall Riots became the catalyst for an entirely new era of LGBTQ resistance, born out of a rejection of respectability, police violence, and discrimination.

STUDENT NONVIOLENT COORDINATING COMMITTEE (SNCC): Ella Baker, Julian Bond, and Diane Nash founded this civil rights organization in 1960 to provide more of a platform for Black students and young people in the larger Civil Rights movement. The SNCC ceased operations in 1976.

SUGARHILL GANG: A Black American hip-hop group, the Sugarhill Gang debuted with their hit song "Rapper's Delight" in 1979.

SUNDOWN TOWNS: Segregated white suburbs, cities, and neighborhoods in the United States that enforced a type of segregation that required strict curfews for Black people and people of color (many of whom worked as domestic laborers and custodians during the day). Violation of the curfews resulted in intimidation, arrest, or mob violence. These mandates extended to people driving through such cities.

SWEATT V. PAINTER (1950): This legal case, which was heard by the U.S. Supreme Court, involved Heman Marion Sweatt and Theophilus Painter, president of the University of Texas Law School. Sweatt had been refused admission to the law school because Texas law prohibited schools from integrating. In 1950, the court held that the Equal Protection Clause of the Fourteenth Amendment mandated that Sweatt be admitted to the University of Texas Law School.

SYLVIA RIVERA (1951–2002): A transgender Latina American LGBTQ rights activist, Rivera was known for her role in the LGBTQ Rights movement in the United States.

TENANT FARMING: *See* sharecropping.

THIRTEENTH AMENDMENT (1865): This amendment banned slavery and all involuntary servitude, except in the case of punishment for a crime.

THURGOOD MARSHALL (1908–1993): A Black American civil rights lawyer, Marshall led the legal strategy of the National Association for the Advancement of Colored People (NAACP), arguing countless civil rights cases before the U.S. Supreme Court that resulted in many landmark victories. In October 1967, President Lyndon B. Johnson appointed him associate justice of the U.S. Supreme Court, where he served until October 1991. Marshall was the court's 96th justice and its first Black American justice.

TOMMIE SMITH (1944–): A Black American activist and track and field athlete, Smith, at age twenty-four, won a gold medal for the two hundred-meter sprint at the 1968 Mexico City Summer Olympics. Smith and his colleague, John Carlos, used the opportunity to protest the 1968 Mexico City Summer Olympics as they received their medals by taking the podium with a reverent lowered gaze and hands raised defiantly in the Black Power salute as the national anthem sounded in the background.

TRANSGENDER: This umbrella term is used to describe people whose gender identity differs from the gender they were assigned at birth.

TRANSPHOBIA: The fear, hatred, disbelief, or mistrust of people who are transgender, thought to be transgender, or whose gender expression doesn't conform to traditional gender roles.

TULSA MASSACRE (1921): The Tulsa massacre took place from May 31 to June 1, 1921, when mobs of white people attacked Black residents, Black-owned businesses, and churches in the Greenwood district in Tulsa, Oklahoma. Estimates for the number of Black people killed range from official accounts of sixty to community accounts of three hundred.

TUSKEGEE AIRMEN: Pilots trained in an experimental program established by the U.S. military after pressure from civil rights organizations. The program lasted from 1940 until 1946, during which time the Tuskegee program trained 996 pilots; 445 of those pilots were deployed overseas. In addition to Black American soldiers, the unit included five Haitians from the Haitian Air Force, a pilot from Trinidad, and another from the Dominican Republic.

TUSKEGEE INSTITUTE: Established by Booker T. Washington in 1881, the Tuskegee Institute is a private Historically Black College or University (HBCU). Home to World War II's Tuskegee Airmen, the campus was designated a national historic site by the National Park Service.

ULYSSES S. GRANT (1822–1885): A white American slaveholder, politician, and military leader, Grant commanded the Union Army during the American Civil War. He became America's 18th president and served from 1869 to 1877.

UNITED FARM WORKERS OF AMERICA: Founded in California in 1962 by Dolores Huerta, Cesar Chavez, Larry Itliong, and Philip Vera Cruz, the United Farm Workers of America is a labor union in the United States that unites farmworkers from the Black, Chicano, Filipino, and Mexican communities.

UNIVERSAL NEGRO IMPROVEMENT ASSOCIATION: The Universal Negro Improvement Association was founded in 1914 by Jamaican human rights leader and philosopher Marcus Garvey. Abbreviated to UNIA, the organization encouraged pro-Blackness, economic self-sufficiency, and the formation of an independent Black nation in Africa for displaced members of the African diasporic community.

VICTOR HUGO GREEN (1892–1960): A Black American postal worker and civil rights activist who, in 1936, began publishing a guidebook called the *The Negro Motorist Green Book* to catalog dining and lodging establishments across America for Black motorists who were barred from segregated establishments on the road.

VIETNAM WAR (1955–1975): Also known as the Second Indochina War, the Vietnam War was a civil conflict of the Communist government of North Vietnam and the Viet Cong against South Vietnam and their ally, the United States. Under President Richard Nixon's orders, the United States withdrew from Vietnam in 1973. Two years later, Vietnam was unified under Communist control. During these long nineteen years, an estimated 3.5 million people, both military and civilian, died as a result.

VIGILANTISM: An action taken by a group or an individual outside of legal authority to issue "justice" is known as vigilantism. Lynching is an example of vigilantism in the twentieth century.

VOTING RIGHTS ACT OF 1965: Signed into law on August 6, 1965, by President Lyndon B. Johnson after decades of advocacy by civil rights organizations, this act outlawed the discriminatory voting practices adopted in many southern states after the Civil War, including poll taxes and literacy tests.

W. E. B. DU BOIS (1868–1963): William Edward Burghardt Du Bois was an American historian, civil rights activist, and scholar who contributed greatly to the landscape of Black American literature with his works *The Souls of Black Folk* (1903), *The Negro* (1915), and *Black Reconstruction* (1935). As cofounder of the National Association for the Advancement of Colored People (NAACP), Du Bois became editor of the organization's publication, *The Crisis*.

WAGNER ACT (1935): Also known as the National Labor Relations Act, this act was written by Senator Robert F. Wagner, passed by the 74th U.S. Congress, and signed into law by President Franklin D. Roosevelt. The main purpose of this act was to establish legal rights and to correct the bargaining power between employers and employees, except in the agricultural and domestic sectors. The act allows employees to safely organize unions and engage in collective bargaining and collective action.

WAR ON DRUGS: Started by President Richard Nixon in the 1970s and bolstered by President Ronald Reagan in 1982, the war on drugs was a policing program that resulted in the criminalization of marginalized people and drove mass incarceration that resulted in a vast increase in the number of incarcerated individuals from the mid-1970s through today.

WHITE FLIGHT: This term applies to the mass movement of white people from urban areas with significant communities of color into suburban areas.

WHITE PASSING: A term used to describe when a person of color is perceived as white, due to having features such as light or white skin, despite being racially and culturally of another group.

WHITE SUPREMACIST: A white supremacist is a person who believes in the racist ideology that white people are superior to and should be dominant over people of color. A white supremacist frequently has anti-Black, anti-Semitic, sexist, and homophobic beliefs.

WHITE SUPREMACY: *See* **white supremacist.**

WOMEN'S LIBERATION MOVEMENT: A political, cultural, and academic movement, the Women's Liberation movement was active from the 1960s through the 1980s. The movement focused on the study and implementation of feminist scholarship and policy in the United States, Europe, and elsewhere.

WOODROW WILSON (1856–1924): The son of religious leaders who leased enslaved people owned by their church, Wilson was a white American politician who served as the 28th president of the United States from 1912 until 1921. Wilson led the United States during World War I.

WORLD WAR I (1914–1918): Also known as the Great War, World War I began on July 28, 1914, with the assassination of Archduke Franz Ferdinand of Austria and ended with an armistice on November 11, 1918. The Central powers, which included Germany, Austria–Hungary, Bulgaria, and the Ottoman Empire, fought against the Allied powers, which included Great Britain, France, Russia, Italy, Romania, Japan, and the United States. Including military and civilian deaths, over 37 million people died as a result of World War I.

WORLD WAR II (1939–1945): World War II began on September 1, 1939, with Adolf Hitler's invasion of Poland and ended on September 2, 1945, following the formal surrender of the Japanese empire. The war was fought between the Axis powers of Germany, Italy, and Japan and the Allied powers, which included France, Britain, and Russia, and later the United States, which entered the conflict following the Japanese military attack on Pearl Harbor in 1941. Including military and civilian deaths, over 60 million people died as a result of World War II.

ZORA NEALE HURSTON (1891–1960): A prolific Black American literary figure, Hurston used the written word in the form of essays and plays to chronicle the realities of life faced by Black Americans across the United States. She wrote many works, the most popular of which include *Their Eyes Were Watching God* (1937), *Color Struck* (1925), and "What White Publishers Won't Print" (1950).

BIBLIOGRAPHY

INTRODUCTION
Bureau of the Census, U.S. Department of Commerce. Report, "We, the American Blacks," September 1993, **www.census.gov/prod/cen1990/wepeople/we-1.pdf**

DeWalt Brown, interview with author, October 2018, Pasadena, CA.

U.S. National Archives. Census Records, 1900–1980, **archives.gov/research/census**

Verna Jean Brown, interview with author, October 2018, Pasadena, CA.

SEPARATE BUT EQUAL
The Constitution Project, "United States of America 1789 (rev. 1992)," **www.constituteproject.org/constitution/United_States_of_America_1992**

Equal Justice Initiative. Report, "Lynching in America: Confronting the Legacy of Racial Terror," 3rd ed., 2017, **https://lynchinginamerica.eji.org/report**

History, Art, and Archives, U.S. House of Representatives. "Revels, Hiram Rhodes," **https:history.house.gov/People/Listing/R/REVELS,-Hiram-Rhodes-(R000166)**

LaCour, Jori. "Know your Louisiana History: Pierre Caliste Landry—First Black Mayor in U.S.," Southern University, **www.southerndigest.com/commentary/article_3cf2ad8a-71c2-11e5-9e53-bb8f38863f0e.html**

Low, W. Augustus, and Virgil A. Clift, ed. *Encyclopedia of Black America*. New York: McGraw-Hill, 1981.

NAACP. "History of Lynchings," **naacp.org/history-of-lynchings**

Nystrom, Justin A. "P. B. S. Pinchback," 64 Parishes Project, Louisiana Endowment for the Humanities, **https://64parishes.org/entry/p-b-s-pinchback**

Onion, Rebecca. "A WWI–Era Memo Asking French Officers to Practice Jim Crow with Black American Troops," *Slate*, April 27, 2016, **slate.com/human-interest/2016/04/secret-information-concerning-black-troops-a-warning-memo-sent-to-the-french-military-during-world-war-i.html**

Snyder, Thomas D., ed. "120 Years of American Education: A Statistical Portrait." National Center for Education Statistics, 1993, **nces.ed.gov/naal/lit_history.asp**

William Jamal Richardson, PhD, interview with author, January 2019, New York City, NY.

BEAUTIFUL—AND UGLY, TOO
Ahmad, A. Muhammad. "The League of Revolutionary Black Workers: A Historical Study," History Is a Weapon, **www.historyisaweapon.org/defcon1/rbwstudy.html**

Beveridge, Andy A. "An Affluent, White Harlem?" *Gotham Gazette*, August 27, 2008, **gothamgazette.com/index.php/demographcis/4077-harlems-shifting-population**

Bruce, Dickson D. *Black American Writing from the Nadir: The Evolution of a Literary Tradition, 1877–1915*. Baton Rouge, LA: Louisiana State University Press, 1992.

Bureau of Indian Affairs, U.S. Department of the Interior. "Our History: Historical Reflections," **www.bia.gov/bia/ojs/careers/our-history**

DuCille, Michel. "Black Moses, Red Scare," *Washington Post*, February 12, 1997, **washingtonpost.com/archive/1997/02/12/black-moses-red-scare/8a6aff0a-6f38-4b50-8c45-77ba7eb5d714/?utm_term=.5ac0f6d9a516**

In Motion. "The Great Migration," **http://www.inmotionaame.org/print.cfm?migration=8&bhcp=1**

The Henry Ford. "African American Workers at Ford Motor Company," February 26, 2013, **thehenryford.org/explore/blog/african-american-workers-at-ford-motor-company**

Hughes, Langston. "The Negro Artist and the Racial Mountain," *The Nation*, March 11, 2002, **english.illinois.edu/maps/poets/g_l/hughes/mountain.htm**

Joshua DuBois, interview with author, November 2018, Washington, DC.

Low, W. Augustus, and Virgil A. Clift, ed. *Encyclopedia of Black America*. New York: McGraw-Hill, 1981.

Maloney, Thomas N., and Warren C. Whatley. "Making the Effort: The Contours of Racial Discrimination in Detroit's Labor Markets, 1920–1940." *The Journal of Economic History*, Vol. 55, No. 3 (September 1995): pp. 465–93, **http://www.jstor.org/stable/2123659**

Shay-Akil McLean, interview with author via email, February 2019.

Tulsa Historical Society and Museum. "1921 Tulsa Race Massacre," **tulsahistory.org/exhibit/1921-tulsa-race-massacre**

I, TOO, AM AMERICA
Buhle, Mari Jo, Paul Buhle, and Dan Georgakas. *Encyclopedia of the American Left*. New York: Garland Pub., 1990.

Ibrahim Muhammad, interview with author, November 2018, St Louis, MO.

Katznelson, Ira. *When Affirmative Action Was White: An Untold History of Racial Inequality in Twentieth-Century America*. New York: W. W. Norton & Company, 2005.

Low, W. Augustus, and Virgil A. Clift, ed. *Encyclopedia of Black America*. New York: McGraw-Hill, 1981.

McElvaine, Robert S. *Encyclopedia of the Great Depression*. New York: Macmillan Reference USA, 2003.

Reed, Lawrence W. "Jesse Owens: Character Makes the Difference When It's Close," Foundation for Economic Education, August 25, 2015, **https://fee.org/articles/hitler-didn-t-snub-me-it-was-our-president**

Richard Brookshire III, interview with author, February 2019, New York City, NY.

Social Welfare History Project, Virginia Commonwealth University. "African Americans and the Civilian Conservation Corps," March 12, 2018, **https://socialwelfare.library.vcu.edu/eras/great-depression/african-americans-and-the-ccc**

LIBERTY AND JUSTICE FOR ALL?
Badger, Emily. "Redlining: Still a Thing," *Washington Post*, May 28, 2015, **washingtonpost.com/news/wonk/wp/2015/05/28/evidence-that-banks-still-deny-black-borrowers-just-as-they-did-50-years-ago/?utm_term=.d8881ddof086**

Cohen, Rhaina. "Who Took Care of Rosie the Riveter's Kids?" *The Atlantic*, November 18, 2015, **theatlantic.com/business/archive/2015/11/daycare-world-war-rosie-riveter/415650**

California Newsreel. Report, "Go Deeper: Where Race Lives," 2003, (accessed on PBS, March 10, 2019). **pbs.org/race/000_About/002_06_a-godeeper.htm**

"'The Color of Law' Details How U.S. Housing Policies Created Segregation," *All Things Considered*, NPR (aired on May 17, 2017), **https://www.npr.org/2017/05/17/528822128/the-color-of-law-details-how-u-s-housing-policies-created-segregation**

Conover, Adam. "The Disturbing History of the Suburbs." *Adam Ruins Everything*. TruTV, October 13, 2017, **youtu.be/e68CoE70Mk8**

Equal Justice Initiative. Report, "Lynching in America: Targeting Black Veterans," 2017, **https://eji.org/reports/online/lynching-in-america-targeting-black-veterans**

Honey, Maureen. "African American Women in World War II," Gilder Lehrman Institute of American History, **gilderlehrman.org/history-now/african-american-women-world-war-ii**

Imani, Blair. "Propaganda, Dehumanization, and World War II," *Medium*, November 18, 2017, **medium.com/@BlairImani/propaganda-dehumanization-and-world-war-ii-d1e965ced9f8**

Imani, Blair, and Monique Le. *Modern HERstory: Stories of Women and Nonbinary People Rewriting History*. Berkeley, CA: Ten Speed Press, 2018.

In Motion. "The Migration Numbers," **inmotionaame .org/migrations/topic.cfm?migration=9&topic=2&tab=image**

Kristina Brown, interview with author, January 2019, Los Angeles, CA.

Lambert, Bruce. "At 50, Levittown Contends with Its Legacy of Bias," *New York Times*, December 28, 1997, **nytimes.com/1997/12/28/nyregion/at-50-levittown-contends-with-its-legacy-of-bias.html**

Low, W. Augustus, and Virgil A. Clift, ed. *Encyclopedia of Black America*. New York: McGraw-Hill, 1981.

Shannon, Jerry. "From Food Deserts to Supermarket Redlining: Making Sense of Food Access in Atlanta," *Atlanta Studies*, August 14, 2018, **https://www.atlantastudies.org/2018/08/14/jerry-shannon-from-food-deserts-to-supermarket-redlining-making-sense-of-food-access-in-atlanta**

Tuskegee University. "The Tuskegee Airmen," **www.tuskegee.edu/support-tu/tuskegee-airmen**

U.S. Army. "Women Airforce Service Pilots (WASP)," **https://www.army.mil/women/history/pilots.html**

U.S. Army War College. "Use of Negro Manpower in War," 1925.

U.S. Veterans Lighthouse. "Guiding Veterans to What They Earned," November 19, 2015, **otherthanhonorabledischarge.wordpress.com/2015/11/19/history-of-other-than-honorable-discharges**

"WASP Official Correspondence," *American Experience*, PBS, **pbs.org/wgbh/americanexperience/features/flygirls-wasp-official-correspondence**

TROUBLE AHEAD
Bureau of the Census, U.S. Department of Commerce. "Black Americans: A Profile," **gov/prod/1/statbrief/sb93_2.pdf**

Bureau of the Census, U.S. Department of Commerce. "Median Family Income, by Race/Ethnicity of Head of Household: 1950 to 1993," *Current Population Reports*, Series P-60, **nces.ed.gov/pubs98/yi/yi16.pdf**

Catsam, Derek Charles. "Tired Feet, Empty Pockets, Rested Souls: Bus Boycotts in the United States and South Africa in the 1940s and 1950s," lecture, Louisiana State University, Baton Rouge, LA, October 31, 2014.

California Newsreel. Report, "Go Deeper: Where Race Lives," 2003, (accessed on PBS, March 10, 2019). **pbs.org/race/000_About/002_06_a-godeeper.htm**

Hughes, Langston. Poetry Foundation. "Harlem," **poetryfoundation.org/poems/46548/harlem**

Long Road to Brown, film produced by Firelight Media, premiered on PBS May 2004, **pbs.org/beyondbrown/history/fullhistory.html**

Low, W. Augustus, and Virgil A. Clift, ed. *Encyclopedia of Black America*. New York: McGraw-Hill, 1981.

Motown Museum curatorial staff, interview with author, October 2018, Detroit, MI.

National Park Service. "Kenneth and Mamie Clark Doll," updated April 10, 2015, **nps.gov/brvb/learn/historyculture/clarkdoll.htm**

Pérez-Peña, Richard. "Woman Linked to 1955 Emmett Till Murder Tells Historian Her Claims Were False," *New York Times*, January 27, 2017, **nytimes.com/2017/01/27/us/emmett-till-lynching-carolyn-bryant-donham.html**

"(2006) Young Blair Imani interviews Dr. Terrence Roberts of the Little Rock Nine," published on July 26, 2017, **youtu.be/ap_XdWIwn0Y**

THE TIME IS IN THE STREET, YOU KNOW
Brown, DeNeen L. "'A Cry for Freedom': The Black Power Salute That Rocked the World 50 Years Ago," *Washington Post*, October 16, 2018, **washingtonpost.com/history/2018/10/16/a-cry-freedom-black-power-salute-that-rocked-world-years-ago**

Civil Rights Movement Veterans. "Civil Rights Movement History: 1951–1968,"**crmvet.org/tim/timhome.htm**

Gregory Hawkins, interview with author via phone, March 2019.

Lewis, John, and Andrew Aiden, *March*. 3 vols. Marietta, GA: Top Shelf Productions, 2016.

Low, W. Augustus, and Virgil A. Clift, ed. *Encyclopedia of Black America*. New York: McGraw-Hill, 1981.

The Martin Luther King Jr. Research and Education Institute. "Beyond Vietnam," **kinginstitute.stanford.edu/king-papers/ documents/beyond-vietnam**

National Museum of African American History and Culture, Washington, DC.

Newton, Huey P. "The Ten-Point Program." In *War against the Panthers*. 1980, **marxists.org/history/usa/workers/black- panthers/1966/10/15.htm**

Odlum, Lakisha. "The Black Power Movement," 2015, retrieved from the Digital Public Library of America, **http://dp.la/ primary-source-sets/the-black-power- movement**

Sadie Roberts-Joseph, interview with author, May 2015, Baton Rouge, LA.

"Soul of a Nation: Art in the Age of Black Power," exhibition at the Tate Modern, London, 2017.

ALL POWER TO ALL THE PEOPLE

Bass, Jack, and Jack Nelson. *The Orangeburg Massacre*. Macon, GA: Mercer University Press, 1984.

Berman, Eliza. "How LIFE Magazine Covered the Kent State Shootings," *Time*, May 4, 2015, **time.com/3839195/life-magazine-kent-state**

"Black History Month 2017: Brad Lomax, Disabled Black Panther," *Ramp Your Voice!* February 17, 2017, **rampyourvoice .com/2017/02/17/black-history-month-2017- brad-lomax-disabled-black-panther**

Brown, Leighton, and Matthew Riemer. *We Are Everywhere: Protest, Power, and Pride in the History of Queer Liberation*. Berkeley, CA: Ten Speed Press, 2019.

Ebony. 30th Anniversary Issue, November 1975.

Feminista Jones, interview with author via video call, October 2018.

Hartman, Steve. "A Look at CBS News' 1967 Documentary: 'The Homosexuals'." CBS News, June 26, 2015, **cbsnews.com/news/ how- far-weve-come-since-the-1967-homosexuals- documentary**

Jamia Wilson, interview with author, February 2019, New York City, NY.

Lorde, Audre. *From a Land Where Other People Live*. Detroit: Broadside Lotus Press, 1973.

Low, W. Augustus, and Virgil A. Clift, ed. *Encyclopedia of Black America*. New York: McGraw-Hill, 1981.

Native Village. "1969 Occupation of Alcatraz" (includes the Alcatraz Proclamation), **https:// www.nativevillage.org/Inspiration-/ Occupation of Alcatraz and the Alcatraz Proclamation alcatraz_proclamation.htm**

Obie, Brooke. "[INTERVIEW] LeVar Burton on Why 'Roots' Still Matters," *Ebony*, October 17, 2018, **ebony.com/entertainment/interview- levar-burton-2013-495**

Roberts, Monica. "The Story of Georgia Black," *TransGriot*, March 5, 2012, **transgriot.blogspot .com/2012/03/story-of-georgia-black.html**

Ruth H. Hopkins, interview with author via email, February 2019.

Timothy Anne Burnside, interview with author, November 2018, Washington, DC.

Vilissa Thompson, interview with author via phone, November 2018.

GLOSSARY

Planned Parenthood. "What's Transphobia?" **plannedparenthood.org/learn/sexual- orientation-gender/trans-and-gender- nonconforming-identities/whats- transphobia**

U.S. Veterans Lighthouse. "Guiding Veterans to What They Earned," November 19, 2015, **otherthanhonorabledischarge.wordpress .com/2015/11/19/history-of-other-than- honorable-discharges**

ABOUT THE AUTHOR

Blair Imani was born in Los Angeles, California. She attended Louisiana State University and graduated in 2015 with a degree in history. Blair is a writer, mental health advocate, and historian living at the intersections of Black, queer, and Muslim identity. In addition to being a public speaker, Blair is the author of *Modern HERstory: Stories of Women and Nonbinary People Rewriting History*. Learn more about Blair by visiting blairimani.com or by following her on social media @blairimani.

ABOUT THE ILLUSTRATOR

Rachelle Baker was born in Detroit, Michigan. She has been a self-taught multimedia artist since she was very young and has been published in *Bitch* magazine and on the cover of Okechukwu Nzelu's book *The Private Joys of Nnenna Maloney*. Rachelle specializes in freehand illustration, printmaking, screen printing, linoleum and wood cutting, comic art, video art, and music. Her artistic inspiration comes from the rich history of comic book art, music video creative direction of the late 1990s and early 2000s, and her upbringing in the Motor City. Learn more about Rachelle by visiting rachellebakerdraws.com.

ACKNOWLEDGMENTS

No author writes a book alone, and no historian can tell history without those who lived it, chronicled it, and preserved it for future generations. It takes a village to write a book, and I could not have done it without the support of my family, friends, mentors, and followers, who keep me going even when I cannot see the light at the end of the tunnel. I am grateful to my parents, DeWalt and Kristina Brown, not only for giving me life but also for encouraging my appetite for curiosity and wonder. My partner, Akeem Omar Ali, for reminding me that this history needs to be told and that I am capable of doing so. My grandmothers, Eloise, Verna Jean, and Marlene, for telling me about their lived experiences and inspiring in me a love of history at a young age.

Rachelle Baker brought this book to life with her vibrant illustrations and amazing creative direction as the illustrator of the book. I am thankful to Grace Bonney for pointing me in her direction.

Patrisse Cullors kept me encouraged throughout this arduous research and writing process. Thank you, Patrisse, for your words of wisdom and for your contribution of the book's foreword.

Thank you to my firebrand editor, Kaitlin Ketchum, for reminding me that there are more stories to be told and more histories to honor. To my publishing team at Penguin Random House and Ten Speed Press, including Kelly Booth, Serena Sigona, Kimmy Tejasindhu, David Hawk, Daniel Wikey, and Monica Stanton. Thanks also to my personal team, including my magnificent manager Mariel Limón and my tenacious agent Sean Lawton, for seamlessly planning my speaking opportunities to coincide with research and interview opportunities across the country.

I am grateful to the many activists, historians, archivists, family members, and friends who have shared time and space with me to make this book possible. Without Kristi Fernandez-Kim and Reina Sultan, the extensive glossary included in this book would not be nearly as thorough or complete. This book would not have been possible without Gregory Hawkins, Craig Stewart, Vernon Brown, Steve Bryant, Debbie Bryant, Donna Hylton, Ani Zonneveld, Feminista Jones, Vilissa Thompson, Naima Cochrane, Adam Conover, Annie Segarra, Mamoudou Ndiaye, Joshua DuBois, LeVar Burton, Mars Sebastian, Lori Rodriguez, Abdi M. Locke Ali, Dr. Caroline Blackman, Taylor Amari Little, Andray Domise, Precious Rasheeda Muhammad, Lanae Spruce, Erin Biba, Terrell Starr, Timothy Anne Burnside, Mariame Kaba, Stephen A. Green, Imani Barbarin, Shay Akil McLean, Ruth H. Hopkins, and Tiffany D. Loftin. I would also like to thank the curators and staff at the National Museum of African American History and Culture in Washington, D.C.; the Motown Museum in Detroit; the Schomburg Museum in Harlem, New York; the National WWII Museum in New Orleans, Louisiana; and the Tate Museum in London. Thanks also to the phenomenal teachers and professors who have grown my love of history: Greg Lupu, Dr. Stephen Finley, Dr. Victor Stater, Dr. Steven Ross, Dr. Lori Martin, and Ms. Sadie Roberts-Joseph.

The stories that comprise this book would not have been possible without interviews provided by the Charbonnet family, the Brown family, the Hawkins family, the Stewart family, the Green family, the Hamilton family, the Muhammad family, the Johnson family, the Hayes family, and the Parks family. Thank you all.

I am grateful most of all to Allah the Beneficent, the Merciful, who grounds my life and my work. Alhamdulillah, ameen.

INDEX

179

This book is dedicated to Ms. Sadie Roberts-Joseph, who often reminded me that "Culture is the glue that holds a people together. Take a step back in time and leap into your future."

Library of Congress Cataloging-in-Publication Data is on file with the publisher.

Hardcover ISBN: 978-1-9848-5692-0
eBook ISBN: 978-1-9848-5693-7

Printed in China

Design by Kelly Booth
Illustrations by Rachelle Baker

10 9 8 7 6 5 4 3 2 1

First Edition